Music and Inspiration

Music and Inspiration

JONATHAN HARVEY

edited by MICHAEL DOWNES

faber and faber
LONDON·NEW YORK

First published in 1999
by Faber and Faber Limited
3 Queen Square London WC1N 3AU
Published in the United States by Faber and Faber Inc.
a division of Farrar, Straus and Giroux Inc., New York

Photoset by Agnesi Text, Hadleigh
Printed in England by Clays Ltd, St Ives plc

A CIP record for this book
is available from the British Library

ISBN 0-571-20025-7

2 4 6 8 10 9 7 5 3 1

Contents

Preface

It was in 1964 that this book took its first form, as a doctoral thesis. Cambridge University, where I was a student, had disapproved of the subject and tried to steer me towards seventeenth-century musicological topics. I refused this temptation rather easily, and made off to Glasgow University where Robin Orr, who had met me at Cambridge and was subsequently to return there as Professor, welcomed me and my subject with open arms. Under his supervision I completed the work, gained the doctorate, and that, for the next thirty-three years, was that. I did try some publishers but they all had the same reaction – although the substance was fascinating, it was not publishable as it stood, but needed rewriting as a book rather than a thesis. When I mentioned to Michael Downes that, preferring not to abandon my composing for some considerable time, I was seeking someone who might do this job for me, his reaction was immediately enthusiastic. He had his own doctoral thesis to finish – on a not dissimilar topic: the musical criticism of Debussy – and a new lecturing post to begin. Nevertheless he rewrote, updated, helped find post-1964 material, and generally put in better order the categories and conclusions of the earlier text, with a skill and energy that could not have been bettered. Nor could my ideas have been more clearly re-formed for the general public. I added things here and there, and went over the new version, but the credit for the presentation of my ideas is largely his. I am deeply grateful to him for resurrecting this little book from the dead.

Introduction

What is inspiration? This is a question most composers have been asked, or have asked themselves, at some stage in their careers – and it is one that has fascinated me for many years. At one level, an answer is easy to provide: inspiration may be defined as that which causes, provokes, forces the artist to create – the catalyst of the creative process. This answer, however, seems to tell the truth but not the whole truth: it is somehow too prosaic to be ultimately satisfying. It excludes an element most would argue was essential to any meaningful definition of inspiration: the element of *mystery*.

When we consider a piece of music that we admire, it is often relatively straightforward to account for many of the decisions made by the composer. We may easily understand why he or she has chosen to write for oboe, harp and strings, for instance, why a particular genre, a suite, perhaps, has been employed; we may deduce, from our knowledge of the composer's biography, why a particular theme or subject matter has appealed to him or her; we may, if we are sufficiently familiar with the historical context of the piece of music under question, be able to comment on the composer's choice of style and idiom for the piece, or on any 'system' of which he or she has made use. All of these are matters concerning which the composer has had to make choices: all

of these choices must have been made as a result of a combination of causes, which may seem more or less apparent,
more or less justified to the listener who considers them.
These causes, however, do not in themselves amount to inspiration, though inspiration may certainly have affected any or
all of these decisions. Inspiration is the *hidden* cause: it may
be almost impossible for the listener to pinpoint its presence
in the finished work, yet without it the work would not
have the individuality for which, presumably, we admire it.
Inspiration is at once the most mysterious influence on the
work, and the most fundamental, because without it the
work's essential identity would be lost.

For many musicians, inspiration is an experience that
has proved very difficult to describe, but relatively easy to
identify. The *nature* of inspiration, as the following pages will
show, has been understood and described in numerous very
different ways. However, the *existence* of inspiration – as a
distinct, coherent, unique experience – is not something that
would be disputed by many of those involved in the activity
of making music. Composers, performers, listeners and critics
share an understanding that 'inspiration' may play a part in
the creation, or re-creation, of a piece of music. This is not to
say, of course, that they will necessarily agree about which
pieces, or performances, are 'inspired': merely that there is a
general consensus about what it means to be 'inspired'.

If the existence of inspiration is generally acknowledged,
then so too is its importance. Most composers would readily
admit that inspiration, at some stage of the compositional
process, is a necessary component of a fully satisfying work.
The more frank among them would admit that there are
some pages of their work which may be technically accomplished and well crafted, but which lack that vital ingredient:
they are the result of diligence rather than inspiration, and no

amount of the former can fully compensate for the absence of the latter. Likewise, performers and listeners often claim that they are able to distinguish pieces of music that are 'inspired', and therefore mysteriously effective, from those that are merely workmanlike. When challenged to say what they mean by this, they may well not be able to supply a satisfactory answer; but this does not lessen their confidence in their instinctive ability to identify the products of musical inspiration.

It is because of this almost universal agreement about both the existence and the importance of inspiration, that statements such as 'Berlioz's claim to be an inspired and natural melodist is irrefutable', and 'neither *Festklänge* nor *Mazeppa* is among the more inspired of [Liszt's] symphonic poems', are generally understood. The idea that a piece of music or an aspect of a composer's style is 'inspired' or 'uninspired' is a commonplace one, even if the process of inspiration that lies behind such claims is not fully understood. (Both these examples were taken, almost at random, from the 1980 edition of the *New Grove Dictionary*, but similar statements may be found in a thousand programme notes, record sleeves and biographies.) Such claims rely on a common agreement both about what inspiration is, and about the inevitable superiority of an 'inspired' work to an 'uninspired' one. Given this agreement, the adjective 'inspired' can serve almost as a shorthand: it denotes a constellation of other qualities that are generally seen as the product of inspiration.

The word 'inspired' is used in such contexts, therefore, to suggest that a work is 'great', 'significant', 'profound', 'innovative' – 'Beethoven's Ninth Symphony is an inspired work' – and its opposite, likewise, suggests related negative qualities. This, it may be argued, is the most common way in which the word 'inspiration' and its derivatives are used in musical discourse today. Such a usage undoubtedly has its advantages, in that a range of musical virtues is intelligibly and economically suggested. However, it also presents dangers: if these words are used without a thorough and precise understanding of what it means for a piece of music to be 'inspired', then they can quickly become clichéd, banal, and ultimately meaningless.

Paradoxically, the word 'inspiration' and its derivatives are both over-used, and insufficiently understood: despite the frequency with which the concept of 'inspiration' is invoked in musical parlance, its precise meaning is seldom considered. There is a need to investigate beneath the popular cliché of 'an inspired piece of music', to consider afresh what inspiration means, to rescue the idea from a too easy acceptance. This claim implies dissatisfaction with the way in which the word is currently used: however, I do not voice this in order to attempt to topple the idea of inspiration from its privileged position in the musical lexicon. On the contrary, it is precisely because inspiration occupies such a central position in the thought of so many composers that an accurate and thorough understanding of its meaning is necessary.

Because the idea of 'inspiration' is often bandied about in a florid and imprecise fashion, it is appropriate to begin this task of reinterpretation by returning to the word itself, cut loose from its accreted cultural connotations. The *Concise Oxford Dictionary* (7th edition) is as good a place to begin as any other; the first three definitions of 'inspiration' contained there are as follows:

1 drawing in of breath
2 inspiring; divine influence, esp. that which is thought to prompt poets etc. and that under which books of Scripture are held to have been written . . .
3 thought etc. that is inspired, prompting; sudden brilliant or timely idea.

The entry suggests three distinct meanings, all of which are particularly relevant to the musical meaning of 'inspiration'. Firstly, and most literally, inspiration is an intake of breath: the necessary prelude to expiration, an essential part of the process that keeps human beings alive. Music, as well as life, relies on inspiration in this most basic sense. No musical utterance can be imagined without such 'inspiration' as its pre-condition: whether literal, as in the singer's or wind player's intake of breath, or metaphorical, as in the string player's preparation of the bow or the conductor's up-beat. Such actions are more than a technical necessity: they are the process by which the body makes itself able to engage in the physical act of making music. In the most basic sense, therefore, there can be no music without inspiration.

The second definition associates inspiration with the divine – and, by extension, with truth. The books of the Bible are a paradigmatic example of an inspired text. It is the presence of the divine, dictating the text, that acts as the guarantor of the text's worth: it underpins its claim to truth. Many poets have drawn on this religious definition of inspiration in an attempt to explain their conviction that their own work contains a kernel of truth that comes from beyond themselves. For such poets, texts that are inspired contain truth, whereas those that are not do not: whatever the intrinsic aesthetic qualities of the latter, they are necessarily of lesser status. Poets are not the only artists who have aspired to 'tell the truth' as well as to create beauty, however. As the final chapter of this book will show, the concept of 'truth' in art has also guided many composers; the religious idea of inspiration as the sole source of truth thus serves as a model for the musician as well as the poet. The idea of telling truth through art has a distinguished philosophical pedigree: Hegel wrote that 'in art we are dealing not with a pleasurable or merely useful plaything, but with . . . an unfolding of truth', an opinion quoted approvingly by the composer–philosopher Theodor Adorno.

The final definition cited emphasizes the suddenness, the unexpectedness of inspiration: an inspired thought is one that arises mysteriously, rather than being the end-product of a train of thought whose steps may be logically retraced. To use a word favoured by Freud, its arrival is 'uncanny'. As we shall see, this mysterious, unpredictable quality marks out the genuine inspiration for the composer, too. Many composers have drawn a distinction between the type of musical decision that arises logically as the result of what has gone before, and the musical insight that appears initially to be unrelated to its surroundings but that turns out on closer inspection to provide a satisfying solution to problems previously experienced. Only the second type of idea can properly be described as inspiration.

Even this brief examination of the word has revealed a complexity to which the standard understanding of 'an inspired piece of music' does not do justice. The experience of musical inspiration, as it will be discussed in this book, encompasses all the meanings cited: it is physical, comparable to the act of preparing to sing or play; it is spiritual, akin to a moment of religious revelation; it is sudden, unpredictable, miraculous. It is all of these things, and yet it is a distinct, coherent experience. Musical inspiration, once experienced, cannot be confused with any other phenomenon.

By this point, various questions about the line of argument that is being taken may well have occurred to the reader. Two possible objections, in particular, should be pointed out and addressed directly here, since the arguments that may be provided in reply are central to the book as a whole. First, the reader may object that the definition of musical inspiration that has been advanced so far compresses a wide range of experiences into a single formula. Would it not be more illuminating to tease out the different shades of meaning of the word 'inspiration', to emphasize the diversity of composers' experiences, rather than proposing a monolithic and therefore necessarily distorted meaning of the word? Second, the reader may accept the argument that musical inspiration is a coherent and unique experience *for the composer*, while wondering whether any trace of this inspiration is discernible by the listener in the finished piece of music.

Both objections are entirely legitimate, and the answers that are provided to them seek to justify the particular approach that I have taken, rather than to negate the importance of the questions raised. The diversity of composers' experience is self-evident: individual composers have clearly encountered inspiration in different ways. Moreover, different nationalities, periods and cultures have constructed different models of inspiration, by which the individual artist is inevitably influenced. I hope that these inflexions of meaning will emerge naturally in the course of this book, as different composers' accounts are examined: the composers' own words testify more eloquently than mine could to the diversity, as well as the profundity, of their experiences of inspiration.

However, I remain convinced that there is a kernel of shared experience that unites all the composers discussed in this book. It was the observation of remarkable similarities between the accounts of otherwise very different composers that prompted me to undertake this study. It is the *persistence* of a particular experience of inspiration – transcending differences of period, nationality, social class, gender, religious and philosophical belief, and musical style – that I am concerned above all to show in this book.

It is for this reason that the book will essentially be a-historical – perhaps trans-historical would be more accurate –

in its approach. Although the idea of 'inspiration' has undoubtedly evolved significantly, even within the relatively limited span of time represented by the music heard in Western concert halls, it is not the primary task of this book to trace this development. Composers from different periods are deliberately juxtaposed, and the continuity between their experiences shown. Such an approach undoubtedly involves forfeiting the chance to place composers in a broad cultural context, but the opportunity it allows to observe surprising links between composers from different periods may offer compensation for this. The reader will be struck at various points both by the similarities *and* the differences between different composers' accounts. However, my primary concern, when constructing the argument, was to allow the congruence between different composers' experiences clearly to emerge.

The second possible objection is more complex: it raises many questions. Does the sensation of inspiration experienced by the composer have any bearing on the finished piece of music? Is there any relationship between the perceptions of inspiration that may be experienced by the composer, the performer and the listener? Is inspiration, ultimately, something that the listener can perceive – and, if not, is it of any real value? All these questions are potentially very interesting; but the truthful response is that they are not matters with which this book will primarily be concerned. To answer them satisfactorily would require a very different sort of book, one that drew on a detailed investigation into the psychology of musical reception, and that placed the figure of the *listener* at its centre. The present book is concerned largely with inspiration as experienced by the *composer*. It identifies the place of inspiration in the *process of composition*, not in the *result* of that process. Others will be better qualified to comment on what role, if any, is played by inspiration in the perceptions of the listener; for the purposes of the present book, the task of elucidating the composer's view of the process is sufficiently daunting.

It is a task, too, that has not previously been undertaken, at least not in any systematic way. There have been remarkably few studies of musical inspiration, and none, to the best of my knowledge, has examined the issue exclusively from the composer's point of view. Louise Duchesneau's *The Voice of the Muse*, published in 1986, deals very interestingly with this issue, but she is at least as concerned with secondary accounts of the process of inspiration, from historians, aestheticians and philosophers, as with composers' own testimonies. Moreover, the composers she cites are quoted in the main in French and German. The present book is the first to make a large body of composers' own writings on the subject of musical inspiration easily accessible to the general English-speaking reader.

This body of writing will form the main focus of the book. This does not mean, of course, that I believe that composers of Western art music have an intellectual monopoly on this subject. Many writers working within disciplines such as psychology, philosophy, literary studies, critical and cultural theory, and theology have developed ideas that relate interestingly to this topic. So too have creative artists working within art forms other than music, and writers on music who are not themselves composers: so indeed have composers working in Eastern musical traditions, or in non-classical musical genres in the West. However, the present book will resist the temptation of drawing extensively on such material. This is partly for an obvious and practical reason: to deal thoroughly with such bodies of writing would require a book many times the length of the present volume, and to deal with them sketchily would be worse than pointless. However, it is also because this is, for better or worse, a composer's book – the apostrophe could be placed in either position: it is a book by a composer about other composers.

Composers' words, therefore, are at the heart of this book. Their letters, journalism, interviews, lectures, articles and books will, where helpful, be extensively quoted: indeed, this book is, in a sense, written from as well as about composers' writings. The intention of this approach is to allow the reader to appreciate the full force of the testimony of the composer concerned, rather than having his words conveyed through the medium of paraphrase or commentary: in this way the singularity of the individual composer's experience of inspiration is conveyed.

This approach will also, I hope, draw readers' attention to the abundance of interesting and original writing composers have produced: this body of writing is of greater importance than is often realized, even by many professional musicians. Literary output, whatever its intrinsic qualities, is not generally considered as an important facet of a composer's work – with certain major exceptions, such as Schumann, Wagner and Schoenberg. The reasons for this are obvious: whereas for a writer it is natural to consider all his output – novels, poems, lectures, criticism, letters – as part of a connected whole, for a musician there is an obvious gap between the notes used as the medium of his most significant work and the words used for his secondary output. The latter will inevitably seem like a poor substitute, since the composer will feel when writing that he is not using his natural medium of communication, however unjustifiable his discomfort may be. The examples I have used, I believe, demonstrate both the range and the quality of the writing of numerous composers: it is not only the obvious examples – Berlioz, Boulez *et al.* – whose literary ability should be recognized.

My reliance on composers' writings does, however, present certain possible problems. Composers, like all creative artists, are frequently less inclined to provide a balanced, objective portrayal of a process than to give a subjective, sometimes polemical account of their own experience: moreover, no subject is more likely than inspiration to elicit such an unbalanced account. This can make it difficult for the commentator to achieve a detached understanding of the experience. This problem is mitigated, however, if several composers' accounts of a particular experience are set against one another: the common ground between their accounts allows us to see how much may be regarded as an essential component of inspiration itself, rather than just the experience of a single composer.

This assumes, however, that composers are willing to tell the truth about their own creative processes. On occasion, they may wish deliberately to deceive, in order to present a more attractive or glamorous picture of themselves: John Deathridge's 'deconstruction' of Wagner's account of his own creative development, found in *The New Grove Wagner*, demonstrates the lengths to which composers may go to present their own creative decisions in a positive light. Wagner is admittedly an extreme example: no other composer has justified himself (or needed to justify himself) in writing in such an elaborate and verbose way. However, the case of Wagner shows the need to be sensitive to the possibility that composers deceive, or at least embroider the truth, in their accounts of inspiration. There can be no ultimate proof that any composer is telling the truth – particularly where this subject is concerned, since the privacy in which composition is usually carried out makes it unlikely that there will be witnesses to corroborate a composer's account. This must make us wary of relying too much on a few sources: again, the breadth of the examples cited here offers some safeguard against the possibility of deliberate deception.

It is perhaps appropriate to comment here on the way in which my examples have been chosen. It is inevitable that the views of certain composers will be cited more than others, but the relative space given to composers by no means implies a value judgement on my part about the worth either of their ideas or of their music. It is simply that some composers have left more material relevant to this subject than others. This is partly a matter of personal inclination: some composers – Wagner, again, is an extreme example – have been more inclined to reveal their feelings about the creative process, while others have shrouded it in secrecy, fearing in some cases that too much openness threatens creativity itself. It is partly the result of economic circumstances: some composers, such as Debussy and Berlioz, have felt obliged at various times to earn money by working as musical journalists, while others have given lectures which have later been published, as part of their work for university music departments, for instance.

To a large extent, though, it is simply a question of what has survived. For example, it is hard to find much information dating from earlier than the eighteenth century about composers' ideas on this subject. This is partly for obvious reasons: letters and publications are less likely to have survived from earlier periods. More fundamentally, though, the composer was generally thought of as a craftsman rather than as an individual creator at this time, so it would not have occurred to many composers to disseminate their views about their own 'creativity', even if they understood their work in these terms. It was rare for composers to publish any literary offerings other than treatises on harmony and acoustics; aesthetic issues in music were generally left to professional theoreticians.

The unavailability of suitable material is particularly extreme in the case of women composers, who are under-represented here, despite my best efforts. This is, of course, the result of the fact that until the post-war years composition was overwhelmingly perceived as a male activity and few women were encouraged to compose. Perhaps more relevantly, even those who did compose successfully lacked the status and public prominence their male colleagues acquired as a result of appointments as conductors, university professors or festival directors. The likelihood of their views being made public was therefore small. Although I have endeavoured to take account of the material that has been published by women composers, the male point of view inevitably predominates. As a result, it has usually seemed most appropriate to refer to 'the composer' as 'he': to refer to 'he or she' or its variants on each occasion would be painfully laborious, while to refer to 'she' would seem perverse given the material being dealt with. Future writers may have a different experience.

While dealing with matters concerning my own procedure, it is perhaps appropriate here to comment briefly on the way in which references have been made to sources of material. My primary concern has been to allow the reader to follow the line of the argument and to observe the connections between the ideas cited, and I did not therefore want to break up the text by giving references for every single comment quoted. However, I realize that many readers may wish to know where they can find more of the writings of the composers whose ideas interest them. The best way to reconcile these two objectives, I felt, was to allow the shorter quotations to stand on their own in the body of the text, but to give the longer quotations in indented text, with notes at the end of the book giving the full sources of this latter category only.

This method is a compromise and, like all compromises, will inevitably seem unsatisfactory to some readers, but I hope that it proves to be the most appropriate way of reconciling the conflicting demands of readability and scholarly protocol.

My final comment about my choice of examples concerns my own position in relation to this book. My personal experience as a composer has naturally fuelled my fascination with this topic, and it would be artificial to exclude that experience from the book altogether. However, my primary aim is not to give a personal account of what inspires me, but to present a view of the phenomenon of inspiration as experienced by composers at large. I do not want to fall into the 'Wagner trap' of distorting the ideas of my predecessors in order to justify an idiosyncratic personal outlook! The body of the book will therefore include relatively few examples from my own work: I have confined my personal reflections on the question of inspiration to a short postscript.

The majority of the book, then, is devoted to the question of how inspiration was understood by the generality of composers working in the period from the early eighteenth century to the present day – with a few earlier examples where it has been possible to locate them. My aim has been to organize and classify this material in such a way that the composer's creative 'field of action' is clearly mapped for the reader.

The easiest way to organize the material would have been according to the historical period, nation or musical genre in which the composer worked, but for reasons that will be clear from what has been said so far, this would have been entirely inappropriate here. Instead, I have chosen to organize the material by presenting a series of different relationships between the composer and the world that receives his music. My emphasis here on the world outside the artist may perhaps surprise the reader: in general, accounts of artistic inspiration focus on the internal psychic activity of the artist, in so far as it can be discerned. This is of course an essential component of the process, but unconscious activity alone cannot produce a successful art work.

The engagement of the unconscious with the 'outside world', in the various guises which that assumes for the artist, is just as important. Numerous composers have stressed the importance of the links – sometimes spontaneous and random, sometimes deliberately sought and contrived – between their own unconscious activity and their personal experience, their efforts to make their music heard, their philosophical or religious ideals. Music is not produced in a vacuum, and musical inspiration does not arise in a mind cut off from contact with the world. The literal dictionary definition of 'inspiration', it will be recalled, involves taking in air from the atmosphere: the outside world is used as a source of the inner process. Despite the popular image of the composer as a solitary, eccentric figure, much of the fascination of his work lies in the way inspiration is produced from the encounter between the artist and the world.

Each chapter of this book will deal with the stimulus to inspiration offered to the composer by a different 'area' of his life, although the division of material into these areas is not absolute, as many examples cross the boundaries of different categories. In particular, the idea of the unconscious remains relevant throughout, since it is the action of the outside stimulus working *upon* the unconscious that offers the most fertile possibilities for musical inspiration.

The book will chart a spiralling trajectory, from the innermost processes of the composer, through his experiences of the world, to his engagement with the absolute. Chapter One will examine the role of the unconscious in musical composition, and composers' strategies for dealing with the necessity and the unpredictability of unconscious inspiration. Chapter Two will turn to the ways in which composers have drawn inspiration from their own experience: composers have consistently acknowledged their conscious need for such external stimuli to inspiration, however much critics have decried such stimuli as irrelevant to 'the music itself'. Chapter Three, moving outwards beyond the composer's own life, will examine the composer's relationship with the various audiences, real and imaginary, that receive his work. How far do composers draw inspiration from the idea of communication with an audience? Many composers have worked with an ideal audience in mind, and this theme will be further examined in Chapter Four, which will focus on the inspiration composers have drawn from their own efforts to make their music reflect an ideal order – political, ethical, philosophical or religious. Numerous composers have believed that music alone can convey an intimation of the divine, of paradise, to humanity; for such composers, this faith in the unique powers of music is perhaps the ultimate inspiration.

Inspiration, then, can come from a number of sources – from within the composer, from the outside world, from the combination of internal and external stimuli – but whatever the source, it remains a recognizable, distinct experience. If this book can convey something of the richness of that experience, alerting the reader to the complexity of the processes involved while simultaneously convincing him or her of their vital importance, then it will have succeeded in its purpose.

ONE

The Composer
and the Unconscious

———

A creative person is always most excited when something happens that he cannot explain, something mysterious or miraculous. Then he is very nervous.

STOCKHAUSEN

The element of mystery – a sense that something miraculous, beyond rational explanation, is taking place – is a crucial component of the experience of inspiration for most composers. Some have found the whole experience so enigmatic that they are not even sure whether they are able to describe it adequately. Varèse, for example, wrote that 'the composer knows as little as anyone else about where the substance of his work comes from', while Delius wrote that 'I, myself, am entirely at a loss to explain how I compose – I know only that at first I conceive a work suddenly, thro' a feeling.' Fortunately for our purposes, other composers have been less bashful in their attempts to account for the experience of inspiration: they have described it in numerous different ways, but the quality of mystery is a common factor in nearly every account.

The need for this element can be expressed in psychological terms, by suggesting that inspiration *requires* the involvement of the unconscious mind: it cannot take place at a purely conscious level. In one sense, of course, it is anachronistic to refer to the 'unconscious minds' of many of the composers whom we shall discuss, since it would not have been a term familiar to those working before the mid-nineteenth century: a composer writing before this time tends to refer to his 'spirit' or 'soul', rather than to his 'unconscious'. This difference of terminology is not important, however, since the continuity between the understanding of inspiration displayed by earlier and later writers is clearly apparent. The twentieth-century notion of 'the unconscious' may be used to describe the hidden, mysterious, irrational activity of the mind without undue distortion of the ideas of earlier composers.

The involvement of the unconscious is a necessary component of inspiration, then: in Wagner's words, 'The poet is the knower of the unconscious.' This does not mean, however, that only unconscious activity can be described as inspiration: this would be an excessively narrow definition. Inspiration is often the result of a collaboration between unconscious and conscious mind, or between the internal workings of the composer's mind and outside influences upon him. Later chapters in this book will consider occasions on which the outside world has acted upon the composer's unconscious: here, though, we are concerned with unconscious inspiration in its purest form. Because of its very inaccessibility – because the external world is almost entirely absent from the process – unconscious inspiration is the most unknown, the least understood part of the composer's activity. As Honegger wrote, 'It is a manifestation of our unconscious which remains inexplicable to us . . . an impulse for which we are not, so to speak, responsible.'

The experience of inspiration is profound, other-worldly, sometimes unsettling, as numerous composers have testified. Many have felt that they have two sharply contrasting lives: the mundane, everyday life, and the mysterious, spiritual life of inspiration. A series of letters written by Tchaikovsky in June 1878 expresses this feeling well:

4

She [the Muse] leaves me only when she feels out of place because my workaday human living has intruded. Always, however, the shadow removes itself and she reappears . . . In a word, an artist lives a double life: an everyday human life and an artistic life . . . Sometimes I look curiously at this productive flow of creativeness which entirely by itself, separate from any conversation I may at the moment be participating in, separate from the people with me at the time, goes on in the region of my brain that is given over to music.[1]

The 'life' of inspiration may proceed in an entirely different direction from the everyday life. As Tchaikovsky testifies, the mood brought on by unconscious inspiration may be wholly different to the mood that external circumstances would seem to dictate: 'Without any special reason for rejoicing, I may be moved by the most cheerful creative mood, and vice versa, a work composed in the happiest surroundings may be touched with dark and gloomy colours.' The composer's existence is perceived as more sharply divided than that of the average human being. This is because his hidden, unconscious aspect is an essential component of his work, and therefore intrudes into the conscious life to a greater degree than is the case for most people.

Musical inspiration activates and brings to light areas of the psyche that are normally deeply obscure, and it is frequently an overwhelming, ecstatic experience. It is so intense that many composers have found it hard to comprehend it as coming from 'within' themselves. Rather, they have described it as an experience that takes them over, of which they are almost passive observers: in Tippett's words, 'It is outside our control . . . it lives us rather than we live it.' Stravinsky's remark that 'I am the vessel through which *Le*

Sacre passed' – suggesting a view of unconscious inspiration as almost a force of nature, overwhelming the innocent composer – is one of the most famous descriptions of this experience, but it is certainly not the only one. Mahler wrote of his Third Symphony:

> Try to conceive a work so vast, that in it the entire world is mirrored – one is, so to speak, only an instrument on which the whole universe plays . . . In such moments I no longer belong to myself.[2]

Sibelius describes a similar experience:

> When the final shape of our work depends on forces more powerful than ourselves, we can later give reasons for this passage or that, but taking it as a whole one is merely an instrument. The power driving us is that marvellous logic which governs a work of art. Let us call it God.[3]

The urge to compose is often experienced as instinctive, physical, unstoppable: the mere human being is left powerless in its wake. Because of its urgency and compulsive quality, it has frequently been compared to the more familiar instincts of the body: eating, breathing, even childbirth. Rakhmaninov, for example, wrote:

> Composing is as essential a part of my being as breathing or eating; it is one of the necessary functions of living. My constant desire to compose music is actually the urge within me to give tonal expression to my feelings, just as I speak to give utterance to my thoughts. That, I believe, is the function that music should serve in the life of every composer; any other function it may fill is purely incidental.[4]

Roger Sessions links the impulse to create music to the earliest instincts of breathing, a comparison that recalls the original etymology of 'inspiration':

> If we consider musical sound from the standpoint of the impulse to produce it, we find that in a very real sense and to a very real degree this impulse, too, is rooted in our earliest, most constantly present and most instant experiences . . . much of our melodic feeling derives from . . . a vocal impulse which first of all is connected with the vital act of breathing and is subject to its nuances.[5]

Elisabeth Lutyens provides an interesting female perspective on this matter. These comments are taken from a letter to her mother, who had urged her to 'let the composer rest' so that she could concentrate on the needs of her family:

> If artists could let their art rest and didn't suffer from the divine discontent which demands expression like labour demands a confinement, there would never have been any art at all . . . It is an urge as strong as the urge to love, labour and have children, which has and will always surmount all vicissitudes.[6]

As these last comments show, inspiration is a very personal, individual, even intimate experience, and the way in which it is described varies according to the character of the composer who experiences it. Despite these differences of inflexion and emphasis, however, there is a considerable unanimity between the descriptions cited: inspiration is not only a subjective experience, it is also an experience that composers have in common. Whatever the other differences between them, composers are united by this fundamental aspect of their creative

7

life: without it, most have felt, they can create nothing of any real worth.

The Need for Inspiration

Most composers have admitted that they require the aid of unconscious inspiration in order to complete a work to their own satisfaction. While some have been reasonably sure that they would receive inspiration on a given occasion, for others it was such an unpredictable visitor that they felt themselves unable to accept commissions in case the unconscious refused to come to their assistance within the required period. Smetana took this view, for example, while Berlioz, though forced like many to accept commissions for financial reasons, disliked doing so because he could not predict the arrival of the inspiration on which he relied.

The need for inspiration has been expressed by composers of very different periods, styles and artistic temperaments: it seems to be an absolute requirement for composition, not restricted to those composers we would immediately expect to rely on instinct. Schoenberg, for example, is sometimes caricatured as a cool-headed, cerebral composer – yet he wrote, considering both the simple and complex in music:

> Only one thing is certain . . . without inspiration *neither* could be accomplished. There are times when I am unable to write a single example of simple counterpoint in two voices, such as I ask sophomores to do in my classes. And, in order to write a *good* example of this sort, I must receive the co-operation of inspiration.[7]

Wagner – whose enormous musical output suggests that he was nothing if not industrious – wrote in a similar vein that

'I must have time and leisure to wait for inspiration, which I can expect only from some remote region of my nature.' Elsewhere, he wrote in relation to *Tristan and Isolde* that 'People say, "Go to work, then all will be right." Very well, in its way, but I, poor devil, lack routine, and if ideas do not come to me of themselves, I cannot make them.' Dvořák took a similar point of view, disdaining the idea that music could be produced to order: 'You imagine composing as altogether too easy a matter; it is only possible to start when we feel enthusiasm.'

Some composers have seemed able to compose fluently in almost all circumstances, but even these admitted that they were bedevilled at times by failing inspiration. This was often due to the nature of the particular piece on which they were working. Mozart, for example, blamed the instrument for which he had been commissioned to write – the 'high-pitched . . . and childish' mechanical organ – for the lack of unconscious aid he felt when writing his obstinate but magnificent *Adagio and Allegro*:

> It is a kind of composition which I detest, I have unfortunately not been able to finish it. And indeed I'd give the whole thing up, if I had not such an important reason to go on with it. But I still hope I shall be able to force myself gradually to finish it. If it were for a large instrument and the work would sound like an organ piece, then I might get some fun out of it.[8]

Richard Strauss is often, if misleadingly, seen as a twentieth-century version of the *Kapellmeister*, able to spin out music almost by craft alone. However he, too, was capable of finding composition irksome if the nature of the piece was not to his taste: he wrote in relation to the *Alpine Symphony*, composed while waiting for the next libretto, that 'I am toiling away at a symphony, which I find rather less amusing than shaking down cockchafers.'

For some composers, the wait for unconscious inspiration has proved frustratingly unpredictable. Mahler, for example, confessed that:

> In art, as in life, I am at the mercy of spontaneity. If I had to compose, not a note would come . . . One summer . . . I made up my mind to finish the Seventh, both Andantes of which were on the table. I plagued myself for two weeks until I sank back into gloom as you well remember; then I tore off to the Dolomites. There I was led the same dance, and at last gave it up and returned home, convinced the whole summer was lost . . . I got into the boat (at Knumpendorf) to be rowed across. At the first stroke of the oars the theme (or rather the rhythm and character) of the introduction to the first movement came into my head – and in four weeks the first, third and fifth movements were done.[9]

In this case, Mahler was in the unusual position of having written the 'interludes' to his symphony – the 'Nachtmusik' second and fourth movements – but not the main substance they were intended to prop up. The way in which the principal material emerged and the speed with which it was eventually completed suggest that it was in some sense already fully formed in the unconscious: the epiphanic moment on the lake was one of revelation rather than invention.

Mahler's gloom in the weeks preceding the revelation suggests a typical experience of compositional sterility: the belief that one has been permanently abandoned by unconscious inspiration. Many composers have reported similar experiences. Haydn was subject to depressions during which he was 'quite incapable of finding even a single idea for many days thereafter'; Brahms 'could fall sick with longing for a new fresh strain'; while Smetana wrote of the world of imagination as 'veiled as though by a mist of depression and pain'. Weber wrote of his experiences of sterility:

> Shall I ever again find a single thought within me? Now there is nothing – nothing. I feel as if I had never composed a note in my life, and that the operas could never have been really mine.[10]

Even Mozart could write that 'If people could see into my heart I should almost feel ashamed. To me everything is cold – cold as ice.' This was written in 1790: a year of uniquely slender production for Mozart, bearing only six works, one of which was the piece for mechanical organ referred to above. For many composers, the sensation of sterility becomes increasingly prevalent as they reach old age. The aged Rameau declared that 'every day I acquire taste, but I have no more genius', while Rossini admitted to a 'state of ever-increasing mental impotence . . . music needs freshness of ideas; I have only listlessness and rabies'. Elgar, too, confessed that after his wife's death, 'The old artistic "striving" world exists for me no more.'

The feelings caused by the conviction that sterility has descended are profound: they may be compared to the belief reported by some religious mystics that they have been abandoned by God and hence deprived of all spiritual refreshment. St Teresa of Avila wrote of one such experience:

> Her reason is reduced to such a state that she is no longer mistress of herself and can think of nothing but her

affliction. Far from her Sovereign Good, why should she desire to live? She feels an extraordinary loneliness . . . all company is torture to her. She is like a person suspended in mid-air, who can neither touch the earth nor mount to heaven. She burns with a consuming thirst and cannot reach the water.[11]

If the composer's idea of inspiration can be related to a religious model, then so too can the opposite: the feeling of sterility and abandonment is experienced by the composer as painfully as by the mystic.

These sensations, however unpleasant, are not without purpose, though: for St Teresa, as for many composers, they *needed* to be experienced and conquered if the true intensity and elation of the union with God/inspiration was to be realized: the periods of greatest sterility have often immediately preceded those of the profoundest inspiration. Composers, too, have suggested that the feeling of illness brought about by sterility is a necessary component of true creativity. Puccini argued that 'sickness' was essential to the creative process – he wrote, prophetically as it turned out:

I am afraid that *Turandot* will never be finished . . . When fever abates, it ends by disappearing, and without fever there is no creation; because emotional art is a kind of malady, an exceptional state of mind, over-excitation of every fibre and every atom of one's being, and so on, *ad aeternum.*[12]

Honegger argues that inspiration, as well as sterility, is necessarily a temporary experience:

Do you really believe that one who creates with the spirit,

who is the individualist type, keeps for any length of time the possibility of surviving, of giving himself to his art, of writing music?[13]

Unconscious inspiration is clearly held up by many composers as a sort of totem: without it there is no 'true' music. When inspiration does arrive, it is treated with reverence and trust, even worship. Countless composers have displayed a belief in the infallibility of the assistance offered by the unconscious. For many, music that was the result of inspiration was inevitably 'right', regardless of whether the composer himself understood the reason for its correctness. Tchaikovsky, for example, wrote that when he experienced the 'somnambulistic condition' of inspiration:

> Everything that flows from one's pen is . . . *invariably* good, and if no external obstacle comes to hinder the creative glow, the result will be an artist's best and most perfect work.

An absolute trust in the rightness of this inspiration was necessary, as Wagner argued:

> Imperious Necessity . . . drives the artist to that fanatical stubbornness wherewith he cries at last: *So it is, and not otherwise!*[15]

Such attitudes are not restricted to the Romantic period, where we might most naturally expect to find them. Schoenberg wrote that 'One must be convinced of the infallibility of one's own fantasy and one must believe in one's own inspiration.' Webern expressed a similar point of view – 'Trust your inspiration! There is no alternative' –

while Stockhausen wrote that 'The essential is what inspiration tells you.'

This absolute conviction in the rightness of unconscious inspiration has been described by many composers as 'instinct': this, rather than the lesser virtues of craftsmanship or intellect, is the essential mark of the creative artist. 'Instinct is infallible. If it leads us astray, it is no longer instinct,' argues Stravinsky; while Debussy, similarly, claims that 'Neither long experience nor the most beautiful talent . . . instinct only – as old as the world . . . can save you.' Ravel, too, argues that the importance of craftsmanship and 'will' (or intellectual control) in the creative process has been overvalued, at the expense of instinct:

> The principle of genius, that is to say, of artistic invention, can only be established by instinct or sensitivity. [There is] a fatal, and relatively modern error, an error that leads people to think that the artistic instinct is directed by the will . . . In art, craftsmanship in the absolute sense of the word cannot exist. In the harmonious proportions of a work, in the elegance of its unfolding, inspiration plays an almost unlimited role. The *will* to develop can only be sterile.[16]

There is a striking consensus among composers that unconscious inspiration – or instinct – is both a necessary part of the creative process and an infallible guide when compositional decisions have to be made. It is exciting, intoxicating, lucid, as seductive and sometimes as fatal as a siren, wayward, elusive, yet essential and infallible to the point of divinity. Unconscious inspiration is the shared experience on which composers rely: how, then, do they seek to ensure its arrival?

Preparation for Inspiration

Despite the unpredictability with which inspiration visits the composer, it has often been believed that it is possible to create conditions in which inspiration is likely, if not certain, to occur. Many composers have noted that their greatest inspirations have been preceded by periods of gestation or preparation. During such periods a certain psychic energy is evident in the unconscious mind: 'a kind of restlessness . . . as if I had gone through an illness', as Egon Wellesz described it. The purpose of this activity is often to create a mental order which is conducive to inspiration, for the unconscious mind dislikes disorder: a conflict may need to be resolved, new data fed in, or a phenomenon (technical or emotional) properly understood and assimilated, before the unconscious can work satisfactorily.

Preparation for unconscious inspiration may easily be divided into two categories. The first consists of conscious activity, deliberately undertaken by the composer in an attempt to stimulate the unconscious. The second consists of activity that is not consciously related to any compositional purpose – indeed, it may not even be related to music. Though it is not undertaken with any deliberate intention of stimulating the unconscious, this activity can none the less be seen as preparatory to inspiration, since the unconscious may draw on it weeks or even years later. The idea the unconscious eventually delivers would not have arisen – or at least, it would not have been the same – if the preparatory activity had not been undertaken. (In the widest sense, a composer's entire life may be understood as preparatory activity, but more will be said in the next chapter on the role played by 'experience' in stimulating the unconscious.)

Deliberate preparation for inspiration may take many

forms. For many, intensive study of some sort is an essential part of the compositional process, even if the evidence of this study cannot be directly discerned in the finished piece. Nielsen, for example, argued:

> The most exacting studies there must be; but they must have been made beforehand. The man who composes with an effort had better not; but he who produces music without ever having toiled should do the same. Many believe in the catchphrase that knowledge and scholarship are detrimental to simplicity, and that, at all costs, they must preserve their souls from the poison of learning and the prose of labour. But it is an undisputed fact that the composers who have written the happiest, sprightliest works have passed through the hardest school (e.g. Mozart).[17]

Dukas took a similar point of view, suggesting that 'It is necessary to know a great deal, and then to make music from that which one does not know.'

Many composers have believed that if such preliminary study is neglected, inspiration will not arise. Honegger used a colourful analogy – and an appropriate one, for the composer of *Pacific 231* – to explain this belief:

> I am like a steam engine: I need to be heated, it takes a long time to prepare myself for real work . . . It is necessary to do much work to deserve this happy trigger . . . to undertake one of these brief voyages into the domain of living music.[18]

Others have shared the view that no real creative progress can be made without much hard work in preparation. Delius wrote that 'inspiration does not come without hard work any more than a crop of corn', while Dvořák confessed that 'This composing is a terrible business before you get down to it, and what a lot of thinking over and study it requires.'

For some, deliberate preparation for inspiration is largely a matter of creating an appropriate atmosphere, in which the unconscious can be freed to operate. Debussy, for example, argued:

> One can never spend too much time constructing that special atmosphere in which a work of art should move. I believe that one should never hurry to write but leave everything to that many-sided play of thoughts – those mysterious workings of the mind which we too often disturb.[19]

Mahler, too, required an atmosphere of concentration and introspection before he could compose seriously; this was the reason why he could compose only during the summer, when he was freed from the demands of his work as a conductor:

> Before [the work] organizes itself, builds itself up, and ferments in [the composer's] brain, it must be preceded by much preoccupation, engrossment with self, a being-dead to the outer world.[20]

For others, preparation may take the form of study, of accumulating information which provides background knowledge for a particular work. This is often particularly important for vocal or operatic music, where the composer wishes to understand the full implications of the text he is setting. Elgar wrote of his preparations for *The Apostles*:

> I first of all read everything I can lay my hands on which bears on the subject directly or indirectly, meditating on all

that I have sifted out as likely to serve my purpose, and blending it with my musical conceptions. Every personality appears to me in musical dress . . . I involuntarily give to each a musical character . . . I do not seek for character motives; they come in all places at all seasons.[21]

For composers of songs or opera, a period of intense meditation upon the text to be set may form an important part of the preparation for inspiration. Castelnuovo-Tedesco wrote that 'When I find a poem that particularly interests me and arouses my emotion, I commit it to memory . . . After some time I sing it quite naturally; the music is born.' Weber was similarly affected by the words to be set, according to his pupil Julius Benedict:

The genius of the composer would sometimes long lie dormant during his frequent repetition of words; and then suddenly the idea of a whole musical piece would flash into his mind like a sudden gleam of light into the darkness.[22]

And a similar phenomenon is described by Grétry:

I read, I re-read twenty times the words that I want to express in sounds; I need several days to warm my head. At last I lose my appetite, my eyes take fire, my imagination rises; then I make an opera in three weeks or a month.[23]

Other composers of opera have concentrated less on the text than on the character or narrative that is to be conveyed by their music. Wagner, for example, gave the following advice to a young composer on how to find a *Leitmotiv* genuinely and mysteriously connected with the character he wished to portray:

Let him take a good look at the one character, for instance, which appeals to him the most this very day . . . At last its lips will part, it opens its mouth, and a ghostly voice breathes something quite distinct, instantly seizable, but so unheard-of . . . that he wakes from out his dream. All has vanished; but in the spiritual ear it still sings on; he has had an idea, a so-called musical Motive . . . It is his motive, legally delivered to and settled on him by that marvellous shape in that wonderful fit of absorption.[24]

For Janáček, it was the entire scenario and emotional content of *Katya Kabanova* that absorbed him:

I was caught by it. You know that terrible and sensitive thing in man, which is without end. Sheer misfortune . . . This had to be made into a work . . . I worked on it about a year. I carried it in my head, pondered – but then, how the writing went forward like a machine.[25]

Henze describes a similarly obsessive involvement with the plot and characters of his *Venus and Adonis*:

My thoughts revolved around the opera unceasingly and obsessively, around its form and style and sound. The writer has to put himself in the position of his characters, feel his way into their psyches and their problems, he has to live the drama, experience the characters' jealousy for himself and suffer the complications of this eternal triangle, if necessary summoning them up from his memory. He must come out of his shell, express his innermost self and yield up everything he possesses.[26]

During such periods of preparation, composers are only

too painfully aware of what they are doing and the relationship of this activity to the piece they will eventually compose.
At other times, though, activity that will lead to inspiration is
undertaken without conscious intent: the connection between
the preparation and the inspiration remains hidden, even to
the composer, until the moment when inspiration is actually
experienced. Stravinsky argued that such preparatory work
was unceasing: 'The real composer thinks about his work the
whole time; he is not always conscious of this, but he is
aware of it later when he suddenly knows what he will do.'
Composition, of course, is such an all-consuming activity
that it is not surprising that a composer should view everything else he does as a form of preparation for his central
creative work. This may be true even when the composer's
secondary activities are of considerable importance in their
own right. Tippett, one of the most socially aware of
twentieth-century musicians, admitted that, for him, 'The
function of creation is . . . primary through all the apparent
manifestations of interest in other social activities . . . the
artist is doing these other social activities to serve, if unknow-
ingly, some still unmanifest needs of artistic creation.'

The knowledge and ideas produced as the result of such
activity are stored in the unconscious; subsequently, and
often unexpectedly, the unconscious may make the relevance
of such activity to a particular composition apparent to the
conscious mind. This can happen in a variety of different
ways: through the memory, through dreams, through the
reordering of mental impressions that naturally occurs after
sleep or a period of rest.

Composers have frequently noted that their unconscious
may draw on events experienced many years previously. This
happens, perhaps, because it is difficult to experience an event
and to understand how it may be converted into musical

form at the same time. Britten gave this difficulty as his reason for refusing to write a piece in memory of John F. Kennedy: '. . . not because in any way I was out of sympathy with such an idea . . . But for me I do not feel the time is ripe; I cannot yet stand back and see it clear.' Debussy, too, was unable to use powerful experiences for compositional ends, until a period of many years had passed: he admitted that 'I have never really been able to do anything whenever anything striking happens in my life; and it is precisely for this reason that I feed on memory.' The composition of *La Mer* provides a good example of this process. Debussy was criticized for writing it when away from the sea, but this objection was irrelevant, as he explained:

> I have always retained a sincere passion for Her [the sea]. You will say that the ocean does not exactly wash the Burgundian hillsides . . . and my seascapes might be studio landscapes! But I have an endless store of memories; to my mind, this is worth more than reality, the charm of which generally weighs too heavily on our thought.[27]

Mental impressions do not, however, have to be dramatic or vivid in order to provide material for inspiration. Fauré noted the way in which his unconscious drew on a store of memories, of which he himself was unaware:

> Something very amusing has happened to me recently. Whilst I was thinking of a thousand different things of no importance whatsoever a kind of rhythmical theme in the style of a Spanish dance took shape in my mind. And this theme just went on its own way, so to speak, without bothering me in any way . . . [it] developed of itself, became harmonized in many different ways, changed and

underwent modulations, in fact it germinated by itself. Obviously, it drew upon the store of my memories ever since I have been in the world – on all those musical textures which have become part of myself. But how strange is this unconscious functioning of the mind, this precise working out of an idea in this way! If I were to write it down it would have a very definite form.[28]

The unconscious is clearly capable of reordering mental impressions to find solutions to compositional difficulties, without any need for conscious thought. Brahms was among the numerous composers who have made grateful use of this phenomenon:

The idea is like the seed corn; it grows imperceptibly in secret. When I have invented or discovered the beginning of a song . . . I shut up the book and go for a walk or take up something else; I think no more of it for perhaps half a year. Nothing is lost, though. When I come back to it again, it has unconsciously taken a new shape and is ready for me to begin working at it.[29]

This process of mental reordering may take place while the composer is asleep: this explains why inspiration is frequently experienced on awakening. Richard Strauss, for example, reported this phenomenon:

Generally speaking we understand by musical inspiration the invention of a motive, a melody which occurs to one suddenly, unsolicited by the intellect, especially immediately after awakening in the early morning or in dreams . . . Am I to believe that my imagination has been at work all night independently of consciousness and without recollection in the platonic sense? My own experience has been this: If I am held up at a certain point in my composition at night and cannot see a profitable way of continuing in spite of much deliberation, I close the lid of the piano or the cover of my manuscript book and go to bed, and when I wake up in the morning – lo and behold! I have found the continuation.[30]

Janáček described a similar experience: 'I fell asleep again. The usual family bustle woke me up in the morning. I hasten to jot down the "inspired" motifs.'

Sleep, in general, has often provided solutions to long-considered musical problems – but dreams have sometimes produced spectacular and unexpected moments of inspiration. As Stravinsky wrote, 'Whatever the role of dreams in relating memory and perception, I believe them to have been the ground for innumerable solutions in my composing activity.' A dream experienced by Mahler while composing his Third Symphony provides a good example of this phenomenon:

A voice called out to me as I slept (it was Beethoven's or Wagner's – I don't keep such bad company at night, do I?): 'Let the horns come in three measures later!' And – I couldn't believe my eyes – there was the most wonderfully simple solution of my difficulty![31]

Numerous other composers have reported being 'given' themes and ideas in dreams. One of the most picturesque examples is Tartini's dream of the devil playing a violin: the 'Devil's Trill' Sonata was the result of his attempt to transcribe the miraculous music he heard. Dreams may provide a stimulus to composition after a gap of many years, too: Ligeti drew inspiration from a childhood dream when composing

Atmosphères, while my own opera, *Inquest of Love*, was the result of dreams noted down up to twenty-six years before the work was completed.

In many cases, it is difficult to identify one particular type of preparation as the source for a particular flash of insight. Inspiration is often the result of several different types of preparation – some conscious and deliberate, others unconscious and random. A good example of such a combination – a collision between careful preparation and a random event, which produces a vital compositional discovery – is given by Mahler:

> In the last movement of my second symphony it so happened to me that I actually searched through the entire world of literature back to the Bible . . . How I got inspiration for this is profoundly significant for the nature of artistic creation. For a long time I turned over in my mind the inclusion of a chorus in the last movement. [His hesitation was prompted in part by a reluctance to draw immodest comparisons with Beethoven's Ninth.] At this time Bülow died and I was present at his memorial. The mood in which I sat there and thought of him who had passed away was exactly the spirit of the work which I was then mulling over. Then the chorus from the organ loft intoned the Klopstock chorale 'Resurrection'! This struck me like a flash of lightning and everything appeared quite clear and distinct within me! The creator waits for this flash; this is the 'holy conception'! . . . had I not already borne this work within me, how could I have had such an experience?[32]

In this case, as in many others, preparation produces inspiration, but in an unexpected way. The moment of inspiration is at first sight random, but on closer inspection it proves to be the result of careful research. The importance of a period of intensive preparation, advocated by so many composers, is amply proved. Such work will not guarantee the arrival of inspiration, but it will make it very much more likely to appear.

The Experience of Inspiration

Musical inspiration is popularly believed to take the form of a sudden flash, a blinding moment of insight which supplies everything the composer needs to complete a given piece. Such moments do occur, of course: indeed, examples of such moments of sudden inspiration have already been discussed, although most of these have arisen as a result of careful preparation. The experience of musical inspiration, however, is generally more complex and varied than the 'thunderbolt' image would lead us to believe. It is rare for a single moment to supply the inspiration needed for an entire work, unless the work is very short: as Boulez writes, 'It is only very seldom that the composer finds himself in the presence of a world that he has glimpsed . . . in a single flash of heightened awareness, a world he then has to bring into actual existence.' It is much more typical for inspiration to be experienced in different ways as work on a piece progresses. The type of inspiration experienced when trying to begin a piece is rather different from that needed when work on a piece is in full flow.

What form does the first inspiration for a piece take? This is a question that fascinates both the lay person and the musician. There are almost as many answers as there are composers, but there is common ground between them: by tracing it, we may begin to understand this most mysterious stage of the process of inspiration.

For a few composers – fortunate ones, perhaps – inspiration is received as a melody or an idea that has already assumed a completed form. Richard Strauss, for example, wrote that he sometimes experienced 'the melodic idea which suddenly falls upon me out of the blue, which emerges without the prompting of an external sensual stimulant or of some spiritual emotion . . . It is the greatest gift of the divinity and cannot be compared with anything else.' On some occasions, the idea that is 'given' is so powerful that it suggests an entire work to the composer. This was how Tchaikovsky's Sixth Symphony began life, for example:

> Yesterday . . . suddenly for some reason or other, everything began to play and sing inside me after a long indifference to music. One theme, an embryo in B major, enthroned itself in my head and unexpectedly fascinated me to such an extent as to make me attempt an entire symphony.[33]

Webern claimed that his first vision of a 'series' for a piece usually carried with it an intimation of how the work as a whole would proceed:

> *How does the series arise?* Our – Schoenberg's, Berg's and my – series mostly arose when an idea occurred to us, linked with an intuitive vision of the entire work . . . if you like – inspiration.[34]

Such 'complete' experiences of inspiration are much less typical than is commonly supposed, however: most compositions proceed from much more modest, less definite origins, or even from nothing at all. Xenakis's account is at the furthest possible extreme from Strauss's:

I have no basic material. In every case I start out of nothing. I consider this to be right because I try to break away from the past . . . I don't force myself into a pre-determined structure, I want to navigate freely.[35]

Peter Maxwell Davies also denies the idea that a piece has a specific point of departure, though for different reasons:

You can be thinking of something entirely different, and then you tune into a process that's going on somewhere. Or it might be a thematic idea, or a purely structural idea . . . Particularly as far as the architecture's concerned, there may very well be something left over that you feel you've not done as well as you might, or that's capable of further extension.[36]

The idea that 'left-over' elements of one piece form the material for the next, thus negating any idea of a definite 'beginning', is shared by Harrison Birtwistle: 'Pieces don't really start: they're part of a continuous process. There are certain things thrown up in the course of composition.'

Other composers have started with nothing, but have found their way in to a piece by a process of improvisation. Even very distinguished composers have admitted to being led largely by chance, the mood of the moment, and a desire to please oneself. Haydn, for example, describes the way in which many of his pieces were created:

I sat down, began to improvise, sad or happy according to my mood, serious or trifling. Once I had seized upon an idea, my whole endeavour was to develop and sustain it in keeping with the rules of art.[37]

27

Schumann, too, did not disdain improvisation, though he argued that it was better done in the head than at the piano:

> It is very nice indeed if you can pick out little melodies on the keyboard; but if such come spontaneously to you, and not at the pianoforte, rejoice even more, for it proves that your inner sense of tone is awakening.[38]

The difficulties of the 'improvisatory' process can themselves be a stimulus to creation, as Stravinsky admits:

> We grub about in expectation of our pleasure . . . guided by our scent, and suddenly we stumble against an unknown obstacle. It gives us a jolt, fecundates our creative power . . . Lucky find.[39]

The process of improvisation can help composers to transform what is initially a rather vague musical idea into a more definite theme. This is the approach taken by Ligeti:

> The naïve initial musical idea can be described as music in the raw state. It would be quite possible for the music to be heard in this state – indeed, it is thus heard when I am improvising on the piano – but the sound, measured against the standards I regard as adequate for the structure and form of the piece, is far too primitive.[40]

A general melodic outline was also the initial inspiration for Edmund Rubbra – who wrote that 'I have a visual impression simply of a musical shape without knowing the actual notes' – and Hindemith, who spoke of 'little motives, consisting of a few tones – tones often not even felt as tones but felt merely as a vague sense of sound'. Oliver Knussen's experience is somewhat different. Although he, too, receives an initial inspiration in the form of a few notes, in his case, every detail of these notes must be in place from the outset:

> I usually have a very specific idea of the sound of one moment, like a photograph, which I then write down. It might be just a pair of chords, or a line, or a bit of layered polyphonic texture, but always instrumentally conceived from the beginning – I can't perceive pitch in the abstract, divorced from time.[41]

For some composers, initial inspiration does not always assume a musical form: it may be an abstract idea or a visual image. Beethoven described how his ideas were only gradually transformed into sound, and later still into specific notes:

> You may ask me where I obtain my ideas. I cannot answer this with any certainty: they come unbidden, spontaneously or unspontaneously. I may grasp them with my hands in the open air, while walking in the woods, in the stillness of night, at early morning. Stimulated by these moods that poets turn into words, I turn my ideas into tones, which resound, roar and rage until at last they stand before me in the form of notes.[42]

Boulez writes that the initial stimulus for composition may take the form of 'an entirely abstract formal idea, quite divorced from any "content"'.

The initial inspiration of many of Stravinsky's works was visual rather than musical. *The Rite of Spring*, famously, took shape from an imagined image, quite unaccompanied by any musical ideas:

One day, when I was finishing the last pages of *The Firebird* in St Petersburg, I had a fleeting vision which came to me as a complete surprise, my mind at the moment being full of other things. I saw in imagination a solemn pagan rite; sage elders seated in a circle, watched a young girl dance herself to death. They were sacrificing her to propitiate the god of spring . . . I must confess that this vision made a deep impression on me.[43]

Tippett's first visions of *A Midsummer Marriage*, similarly, were not specifically connected to any musical idea, but consisted of a dramatic scene: man rebuffed by girl. None the less, his vision was sufficiently definite to allow him accurately to determine whether later ideas did or did not belong to this particular conception. For other composers, the initial idea may even be a combination of the visual and the aural. Brian Ferneyhough, for example, stated:

The first sensation, the experience which begins to persuade me that I am actually going to write a piece, is very often a cross between a tactile, a visual, and an aural one. That is, I tend to perceive a mass, almost a tangible sculptural or sculpted mass, in some sort of imagined space, which is made up of these various elements.[44]

The variety of starting points from which composers have worked must make us wary of applying too narrow a definition of 'inspiration', or of equating it too easily with a musical idea. Moreover, inspiration is certainly not confined to the earliest stages of the compositional process. It has at least as important a part to play in encouraging ideas to develop, and to give rise to further ideas. Tchaikovsky's well-known remarks describe the often ecstatic nature of this process:

I would try vainly to express in words that unbounded sense of bliss that comes over me when a new idea opens up within me and starts to take on definite form. Then I forget everything and behave like one demented. Everything inside me begins to pulse and quiver: I hardly begin the sketch before one thought begins tumbling over another. There is something somnambulistic about this condition. "On ne s'entend pas vivre." It is impossible to describe such moments.[45]

Janáček described a similarly inexorable process of musical growth:

An idea, when it arises, acknowledges neither spare time nor time that is tied down. It wakes you from sleep, slows or quickens your step during a walk . . . As the idea grows, you lose yourself.[46]

As the musical work begins to take shape, the composer typically becomes increasingly absorbed by the experience. He draws on an ability to focus on the work in progress, an ability that Carlos Chávez argues is essential, if inspiration is to be maintained:

Inspiration is a state of spirit, a state of mind, and – why not? – a state of ecstasy (in its rigorous sense of being carried away), in which all the mental, psychic and spiritual forces of the individual concur intensely for a single purpose, that of creating, composing or investigating in a total concentration of faculties in a given direction. We do not call all cases of concentration inspiration, but all cases of inspiration involve concentration.[47]

For many composers, this process of concentration requires them to cut themselves off completely from the everyday world, shutting the door firmly behind them: they become absorbed in the work in progress.

There are numerous accounts of this process of absorption. Haydn declared in an interview given in his old age that:

> Usually musical ideas are pursuing me, to the point of torture, I cannot escape them, they stand like walls before me. If it's an *Allegro* that pursues me, my pulse keeps beating faster, I can get no sleep. If it's an *Adagio*, then I notice my pulse beating slowly. My imagination plays on me as if I were a clavier.[48]

Mozart was perhaps the most musically absorbed composer who ever lived: he found it possible, indeed necessary, completely to ignore the outside world. He wrote in a letter that 'You know that I am soaked in music, that I am immersed in it all day long, and that I love to plan works, study and meditate.' Each work threatened to devour him: when composing *Idomeneo*, he wondered whether he would 'turn *into* the 3rd Act, I'm so obsessed with it'.

Other composers have found that work on an opera is peculiarly capable of drawing them into an internal world. Debussy wrote, when composing his only completed opera:

> Pelléas and Mélisande are my only little friends just now; besides, perhaps we are beginning to know each other too well and continually tell stories whose endings we know perfectly; and then, to finish a work, isn't this a little like the death of someone you love?[49]

He found the world of imagination that engulfed him during

this composition almost self-sufficient. The same was true to an even greater extent of his work on an opera based on Edgar Allan Poe's *The Fall of the House of Usher*. Although it was never completed, this idea dominated his final years: at one point he wrote that he would not be surprised to see the sister of Roderick Usher coming through his study door. Rimsky-Korsakov, too, found when composing an opera that everything around him seemed to belong to the 'world' of the piece. He wrote of one summer holiday:

> Everything was somehow in peculiar harmony with my pantheistic frame of mind at the time and my passion for the subject of *Snyegorochka* [*Snow Maiden*]. A thick crooked knot or stump overgrown with moss appeared to me the wood demon or his abode; the forest Volchinyets – a forbidden forest; the bare Kopytyets hillock – Yarilo's mountain; the triple echo heard from our balcony – seemed voices of wood sprites or other supernatural beings.[50]

The composer frequently becomes so absorbed in the piece of music that it begins, for him, to constitute a separate, self-sufficient world. This is proved by the way in which composers write that they 'live in' or 'inhabit' their music: Beethoven wrote that 'I live entirely in my music', while Wagner wrote of *Tristan* that 'I am living wholly in this music . . . I live in it eternally.' For Chopin, composition was such an all-consuming process that he lost any sense of the progress of time in the outside world: 'How often I take night for day and day for night; how often I live in my dreams, and sleep in the daytime.' Many composers have had the sensation that they can hear only the piece in which they are currently absorbed. Gluck wrote of *Alceste* that 'For a month now it has given me no sleep; my wife is in despair: it seems to me that I have a hive of bees buzzing in my head.' Elgar, quoting a theme from *Gerontius*, declared, 'This is what I hear all day – the trees are singing my music – or have I sung theirs? I suppose I have.'

Many composers, indeed, come to prefer this 'world' of the unconscious to the 'real', outside world, finding it richer and more exciting. This can, however, become a depressing, if not psychologically dangerous, tendency. Tippett warns of the possibility that 'The artist who has to animate his imaginative powers in order to create thereby endangers partially or altogether at times his sense of reality.' Xenakis, as if to prove his point, declares that 'I don't live in reality. It's as if I'm in a well. Because of my weakened senses I can't immediately grasp the surrounding world.' The unpleasant aspect of this tendency is particularly acute when the composer is attempting to create music that expresses sadness or fear. From personal experience, I remember well the threateningly heavy cloud that hung over my life when I was composing the descent to 'hell' in *Inquest of Love*, and the depression experienced when composing the long electronic 'descent' section of *Madonna of Winter and Spring*.

If such absorption is occasionally unpleasant, then most composers have also found it necessary if inspiration is to be maintained. As the end of the work approaches, the experience of inspiration changes. The composer senses his goal being approached, dimly at first, then with more certainty: inspiration, at this stage, is less a moment of sudden revelation than a constant, continuous process. The compositional process, here, often seems like a discovery, the gradual clarifying of a vague idea to the point where it may be identified as the long-sought goal. This type of inspiration was described by Roger Sessions, speaking of Beethoven's composition of the 'Hammerklavier' Sonata in particular:

The inspiration takes the form . . . not of a sudden flash of music, but [of] a clearly envisaged impulse toward a certain goal for which the composer was obliged to strive. When . . . this perfect realization was attained, however, there would have been no hesitation – rather a flash of recognition that this was exactly what he wanted.[51]

Beethoven's sketch books are perhaps the most eloquent witness to the idea of inspiration as a gradual, 'clarifying' process: in them we can trace the emergence not only of themes but of entire structures, gradually becoming more and more crystalline.

For composers who, like Beethoven, are inspired in this way, composition is perhaps less a process of *creation* than one of *discovery*. This understanding of the compositional process has been particularly prevalent in the twentieth century, as composers' accounts testify. Stravinsky wrote that 'I usually recognize my find', suggesting a view of the work as an object long striven for and finally identified, not newly made. Other twentieth-century composers have stressed the progressive nature of inspiration, likening it to the gradual discovery of an object. Britten once likened composition to approaching a house slowly in a mist, while Wellesz wrote that 'It is like approaching a tree in the mist; at first we see only the outline, then the branches, and finally the leaves.' Honegger employs a very similar metaphor:

Imagine a building that you are constructing, of which you perceive vaguely at first the general plan and which becomes progressively more and more precise in the mind . . . I look first for the contour, the general aspect of the work. Let us say, for instance, that I see outlined in a very thick mist a sort of palace. Contemplation gradually dissipates this

mist and allows one to see a little more clearly. Sometimes
a ray of the sun comes and lights up a wing of this palace
under construction; this fragment becomes my model.[52]

When finally satisfied with the work or passage in progress,
he not only recognized it but also realized that 'There was no
other solution.'

Unconscious inspiration, therefore, has a part to play at
every stage of the compositional process. It does not simply
provide an initial impulse, or a clever solution to a technical
difficulty; it guides the composer's work throughout. It is the
ability to transform the initial idea into a satisfactory whole
that marks out the true composer, and the true inspiration, as
Schoenberg argued:

> The work of art is conceived whole. The inspiration is not
> the theme but the whole work . . . A creator has a vision
> which has not existed before this vision. In fact the concept
> of creator and creation should be formed in harmony with
> the Divine Model; inspiration and perfection, wish and ful-
> filment, will and accomplishment coincide spontaneously
> and simultaneously.[53]

The importance of unconscious inspiration, in guiding the
composer's path from idea to realization, is central. The role
of the unconscious, therefore, can never be usurped; however,
it can be modified. A composer's inspiration is significantly
affected by his experience of life, and by his relationship with
the outside world: these factors mark the unconscious, and
through it, the finished piece of music.

TWO

The Composer
and Experience

———

You could see art, artistic creation, as a soup constantly
simmering in a cauldron. The taste of the soup depends
on what you have put in it; the broth simmering over
the fire is the artist's potential and what you put into it
are the experiences.

LIGETI

The relationship between the artist's unconscious and the experiences he undergoes is a delicate and complex one. Neither, on its own, can create a work of art. The artist's unconscious cannot work in isolation from the rest of the artist's life: that, to pursue Ligeti's analogy, would be like expecting a tasty soup from the stock alone, with no fresh ingredients being added. Nor does experience alone produce a meaningful work of art: that would be like trying to produce a satisfactory soup by simply combining raw ingredients, without taking the time to cook them. Ligeti's culinary conceit may, by his own admission, be 'slightly forced': however, it manages succinctly to convey a sophisticated and precise view of the relationship between the artist's unconscious creativity on the one hand and his experiences of life on the other. He understands that musical inspiration is most often produced as a result of experience stimulating the individual artist's unconscious into creativity. The range of ingredients that may influence the finished art work is wide: it encompasses collective as well as personal experiences, mundane events as well as profound ones.

A serious artist does not, of course, simply 'express' his experience in his work in the same form as that in which he found it: this is perhaps even more true for music than for other art forms. Rather, experience is filtered through the composer's mind, both at a conscious and at an unconscious level: only forms of experience that have a particular resonance for him will contribute to the creative process. Even when specific sources of inspiration may be identified for a particular piece of music, these elements are never simply transcribed: the composer's involvement in responding to and shaping the initial stimulus is always evident. External stimuli become part of the internal psychic reality: one catches a glimpse of oneself in things that excite or have significance for one.

Many composers have recognized that the nominal source of a piece's inspiration is of less importance than the echoes it evokes for the musician. Ravel wrote in relation to *Daphnis and Chloë*, for example, that he was 'less concerned with archaism than with the Greece of my dreams'. The factual Greece is only a background to the fantasy of Greece which is of immense importance to the composer. Greece has served to invoke a psychic reality already within the composer and bring it to light. Likewise, Richard Strauss created in *Der Rosenkavalier* a musical representation of a fantasy of mid-eighteenth-century Vienna. It did not matter that the main musical device employed by the opera – the waltz – was a form that had enjoyed its heyday at least a hundred years after the period in which the libretto was set. The waltz – like the ideas of romance, elegance and sophistication in Hofmansthal's libretto – represented an ideal image of Vienna which was a much greater inspiration to Strauss than the reality could ever have been. When we say that a composer has been inspired by an experience, therefore, we mean that he has translated it into the psychological domain, identified elements of it that have a personal resonance for him. The presence of 'humanity', within and alongside the external experience, is vital, however difficult this quality is to define.

In my own work as a composer, I have noticed that a range of experiences may prompt me into creativity: from my point of view, such experiences subsequently form part of the particular 'flavour' of the work concerned. Experience can stimulate composition in a variety of ways. For example, thinking about extra-musical subjects that are exciting will often generate music, which then becomes associated with that 'excitement': for me, therefore, the music remains linked to my feelings about the subject. Secondly, because composing is a rather slow activity, many thoughts and associations flash through the mind during the composition of each moment: these too may 'stick to' the music thereafter. A sequence of musical logic may throw up a chord which, as I write it down over some thirty seconds, suddenly reminds me of a moment in a Monteverdi opera, for instance. Thus that moment, for me, will always contain pathos, love, death or whatever the Monteverdi reference might have contained. Music thus has an ability to make complex, wide-ranging connections, often in a more economical and poignant way than language.

The listener to my music is, of course, entitled to object here that whatever the associations of a particular moment for me, there is no guarantee at all that these associations will be transmitted to him or her. The chord that, for me, will forever be linked with Monteverdi, may remind one listener of Mozart, another of Messiaen; for another listener still, the moment may be associated with no composer other than Jonathan Harvey. For each of these three listeners, the associations of the particular moment will be very different: and for all of them, their experience of the moment will be very different from my own. Logically, therefore, the connections I have mentioned do not belong to the music itself: only to my particular experience of composing it.

This point was considered by Ives in his 'Essays Before a Sonata', which were written in order to demonstrate to the listener how he had transformed his experience of reading four Transcendentalist writers into the four movements of his 'Concord' Sonata. For Ives himself, individual moments of the piece had quite clear associations. However, he freely admitted that these might not be transmitted to the listener:

> That which the composer intends to represent as 'high vitality' sounds like something quite different to different listeners. That which I like to think suggests Thoreau's submission to nature may, to another, seem something like Hawthorne's 'conception of the relentlessness of an evil conscience' – and to the rest of our friends, but a series of unpleasant sounds. How far can the composer be held accountable? Beyond a certain point the responsibility is more or less undeterminable.[1]

The questions considered by Ives form part of a familiar debate about whether music is capable of *expressing* anything beyond itself: although this issue has been discussed for almost as long as music itself has been created, it is still capable of arousing fierce controversy, both among professional theorists and among interested listeners. The arguments on both sides of the debate have been extensively rehearsed elsewhere, and it would be both impractical and unnecessary to attempt to deal with them here. For our present purposes, it does not matter whether details of the composer's experience are transmitted to the listener: as I made clear in the introduction, my concern is to locate inspiration in the process of composition, not in the end result of that process. What matters here is not whether music can *convey* anything of its composer's experiences, but whether those experiences *influenced* the compositional process.

As I stated above, my own practice as a composer has been influenced by the experiences I have undergone, at a variety of levels – and the majority of composers seem to have felt the same way, as the examples to be discussed will demonstrate. For the moment, Schumann's eloquent defence of the importance of extra-musical stimuli to the compositional process may serve to illustrate the point:

We must not too lightly estimate outward influences and impressions . . . The greater the number of elements cognate in music, which the thought or picture created in tones contains, the more poetic and plastic the expression of the composition. And the more imaginatively or keenly the musician grasps these, the more his work will move and uplift us. Why should not the thought of immortality have seized Beethoven during his improvisations? Why should not the memory of a great fallen hero have excited a composition in him? Why could not the memory of bygone, happy days have inspired another? . . . Italy, the Alps, the sight of the ocean, spring, twilight – has music indeed not told us anything of these?[2]

Composers have drawn inspiration from a multitude of different experiences, ranging from the most mundane to the most profound.

The Everyday World

Composers have often proved capable of drawing musical inspiration from the most prosaic of phenomena. Everyday objects, for example, might seem the most unlikely source of musical inspiration, unless they have a particularly poignant personal association. However, even the most banal collections of artefacts might suggest a musical idea to an alert composer. Weber, for example, found inspiration for a march in *Oberon* by seeing upturned tables and chairs in a café: 'Look there . . . does that not look exactly like a great triumphal march? *Donnerswetter!* What chords there are for the trumpets! I can use that!' Messiaen, too, was inspired by a random collection of shapes, noting that the sharp forms of stalactites in a grotto 'determine a very exact musical response'. Stravinsky asks himself (through the medium of Robert Craft), 'Has music ever been suggested to you by, or has a musical idea ever occurred to you from, a purely visual experience of movement, line or pattern?' His reply – 'Countless times, I suppose' – suggests that he has had in his composition an almost unconscious liaison with the world of shapes and movement. On a more abstract level, when Stockhausen was planning the main outlines of the 'envelopes' for each group in *Gruppen* for three orchestras (1957), he worked in a room in Paspels bei Chür in Switzerland that looked out on to distant mountains. He used their contours to determine the shapes of these envelopes.

The colours of physical objects, as well as their forms, have played a part in stimulating certain composers. Grétry, for example, found that:

> The lowered or flattened tones have the same effect on the ear as dark, gloomy colours on the eye; the raised or sharp tones have, on the contrary, an effect similar to that of the bright, lively colours. Between these two extremes we find, in music as well as in painting, all the colours which are appropriate to the description of varied emotions and characters.[3]

Arthur Bliss recorded that when composing he always

experienced a play of colour sensations, and that such a feeling was particularly vivid when composing his *A Colour Symphony*; nearer our own time, Ligeti has been influenced on many occasions by associations between colours and sounds. No composer, however, experienced this type of synaesthesia more strongly than Skryabin. Throughout his career, he associated a specific colour with each note. For the most part, these associations were kept as a private 'background' to his music; in *Prometheus*, however, he attempted to convey them directly to the listener. He wrote a part for a 'colour organ', a device that was supposed to bathe the entire auditorium in a light whose colour reflected the prevailing harmony of the music: where the harmony changed very quickly, therefore, so too did the lighting required. Of course, Skryabin's ideas went well beyond what the technology of his day could provide, and even more recently, financial constraints have prevented the piece from being realized as he would have wished, except on a very few occasions.

Skryabin's ideas were the result of a peculiarly *fin-de-siècle* hypersensitivity to the links between sound and colour, and indeed between music and the natural world as a whole. If his synaesthesia was a personal idiosyncrasy, however, his belief in the existence of a mysterious association between music and nature has been shared by many other composers. Rameau, who was the foremost musical theorist of his day as well as France's leading operatic composer, published a *Treatise of Harmony Reduced to its Natural Principles*, whose purpose was to show that all harmonic principles could be related to natural physical phenomena. The ideal of imitating nature has influenced many composers at an illustrative level, too: Handel's *Israel in Egypt* and Haydn's *The Seasons* were early and influential examples of such 'tone-painting'.

The most famous piece inspired by nature is, of course, the 'Pastoral' Symphony, whose composer wrote:

> No one could love the country as much as I do. For surely woods, trees and rocks produce the echo which man desires to hear.[4]

Beethoven argued that his piece was 'more feeling than tone-painting'; for him, the expression of man's kinship with nature was more important than the imitation of natural phenomena.

Beethoven's attitude has proved influential: Romantic and twentieth-century composers have followed him in their concern to explore the feelings that nature awakes within them. Schumann, for example, denied that any part of the 'Spring' Symphony aimed to imitate natural phenomena, but claimed that the piece as a whole was imbued with the sense of spring:

> I wrote this symphony at the end of winter with a spring-like urge . . . I do not attempt to depict or to describe anything in it; but I do believe that the season in which the symphony was born influenced its structure and helped make it what it is.[5]

Mendelssohn, too, found echoes of his inner musical feelings in nature: he loved 'the serenity of nature, which is itself mostly music', and describes the Alban hills as 'a lovely vision . . . No lack of music there; it echoes and vibrates on every side.' Debussy – who sharply criticized the 'Pastoral' Symphony for its 'misunderstanding . . . between man and nature' – believed that music was connected to nature in a mystical, holistic way. Music, for him, did not show its allegiance to nature by imitating its surface phenomena, but by attempting to portray the effect that nature as a whole had on the composer:

> Does one render the mystery of the forest by recording the heights of the trees? It is more a process where the limitless depths of the forest give free rein to the imagination.[6]

Many composers have been acutely self-aware about their need to experience nature: some have deliberately remembered and stored their feelings in a mental notebook of strange and exciting experiences, to be expressed later in music. Busoni writes of Trient:

> The perspective at the end of the valley awakens a feeling of longing, and seen in the morning or even at sunset it makes a great impression on the emotions. I believe, if it is properly absorbed by the soul, it should be productive to the creative flow (later on).[7]

Ravel, likewise, wrote of his journey on a steamer along the Rhine:

> Towards evening we went down to see the factories. How can I tell you about these great smelting castles, these great incandescent cathedrals and the wonderful symphony of travelling belts, whistles and terrific hammerblows in which you are submerged? And everywhere the sky is a scorching, deep red. On top of it all a storm broke . . . How much music there is in all this! – and I certainly intend to use it.[8]

Certain composers have been influenced not merely by the

experience of natural phenomena, but by the actual acoustical properties of nature, of the open air. The depictions of bands moving through the parks in Debussy's *Fêtes* and Ives's symphonies spring immediately to mind. Mahler provides a particularly interesting example of this phenomenon. He was fascinated by the way in which the open air allowed a huge variety of sounds to combine, while each maintained its distinctness: some of the most adventurous passages in his music find their origins in this experience. Natalie Bauer-Lechner recalled a trip to a country fête with the composer:

> Not only were innumerable barrel-organs blaring out from merry-go-rounds, see-saws, shooting galleries and puppet shows, but a military band and a men's choral society had established themselves there as well. All these groups, in the same forest clearing, were creating an incredible musical pandemonium without paying the slightest attention to each other. Mahler exclaimed: 'You hear? That's polyphony, and that's where I get it from! Even when I was quite a small child, in the woods at Iglau, this used to move me so strangely, and impressed itself upon me. For it's all the same whether it resounds in a din like this or in a thousandfold bird song, in the howling of the storm, the lapping of the waves, or the crackling of the fire. Just so – from quite different directions – the themes must enter; and they must be just as different from each other in rhythm and melodic character.'[9]

Donald Mitchell argues that passages in, for example, the Third Symphony find their origins in experiences such as this: Mahler's willingness to write passages in which sounds appeared from different directions, with no apparent relationship between them, was in fact derived from his perceptions of the chaotic collection of sounds he found in his everyday experience of nature.

The last few examples – Ravel, Debussy, Ives, Mahler – have taken us beyond the world of nature as strictly understood, and into the field of human activities. Of course, almost every aspect of human life has at some time or another acted as a creative stimulus to composers. For some, the patterns and intonations of human speech have been an essential musical source. Janáček, for example, believed that each intonation that could be found in human speech had a specific meaning. If these could be translated into music, then a vocal or dramatic piece would be able to convey a much more specific message:

> For me, music emanating from instruments, whether in the works of Beethoven or of any other composer, contains little real truth . . . when anyone speaks to me, I listen more to the tonal modulation in his voice than to what he is actually saying, what he is like, what he feels, whether he is lying, whether he is agitated or is merely making conventional conversation. I can even feel, or rather hear, any hidden sorrow. Life is sound, the tonal modulation of the human speech. Every living being is filled with the deepest truth. That, you see, has been one of the main needs of my life. I have been taking down speech melodies since the year 1897. I have a vast collection of notebooks filled with them: you see they are my window through which I look into the soul – but this is what I should like to emphasize: they are of the utmost importance to dramatic music.[10]

Janáček was not the only composer who believed that the intonations of everyday speech contained the key to music's expressive powers. Musorgsky's operas, particularly *The Marriage,* were unprecedented in the exactness with which their vocal rhythms recorded exact speech, while Wagner expressed the same desire, though as usual in more theoretical terms:

> The musical instrument is an echo of the human voice, but so constituted that we can only detect in it the vowel resolved into the musical Tone, like that *Ur*-tone of all human speech.[11]

In the twentieth century, composers have recorded many more aspects of human life in music, often with the aid of technology, which permits a more exact reproduction of 'life' than ever before. Some have used recording techniques to achieve a synthesis between music and the cadences of actual speech: Steve Reich's *The Cave,* for example, takes numerous recordings of verses read from the Old Testament, altering them electronically and using their rhythmic and melodic patterns as the basis of a musical composition. Others have incorporated recorded reproductions of the environment in their work: for example, Stockhausen, in *Hymnen*; Lansky in works such as *Quakerbridge* (which was recorded at a shopping mall); and Cage, in *Roaratorio*, which requires recordings to be taken of everyday life in every place in Ireland that was mentioned in Joyce's *Finnegans Wake*. For such composers, it is not only ideas, but sound itself, that can be drawn from the world of human activity.

If these composers have been influenced by human life in general, then others have drawn inspiration from specific events, finding deep resonances between the event itself and their own emotions. Janáček, for example, wrote a piano sonata inspired by the poignant events he had witnessed on a particular day, *1.x.1905*. Britten was frequently influenced by external events: he made a visit to the Belsen death camps, the resonances of which were felt in numerous works, including *The Holy Sonnets of John Donne*, and his own conscientious objection during the Second World War undoubtedly contributed to his self-identification with the tortured idealist Peter Grimes. The power of external events to inspire music is particularly strong when the events coincide in some way with an idea or theme that already interests the composer. Thea Musgrave describes the effect of hearing the news of a mining disaster in Germany, shortly after she had been working on music for a television play about a mining community in nineteenth-century Scotland:

> This strange coincidence gave rise to various thoughts, and it occurred to me that the story of the play . . . could be expanded into a much larger social context . . . Here, I felt, were the tensions, both social and personal, that could be the basis for an exciting and meaningful libretto. At the time I had no particular intention of writing an opera, though it was a medium that much attracted me. Fired by the idea, I postponed all other work and devoted myself to it entirely.[12]

Some composers are politically committed to creating music that reflects contemporary events: in recent years, this has been the case for Marxists such as Hans Werner Henze, Luigi Nono, and Helmut Lachenmann, who wrote that 'The experience of the Beautiful is indissolubly connected with making perceptible the social contradictions in our reality.' The commitment to representing contemporary events was also, of course, felt by the composers of Soviet Russia, though in Soviet society composers' choices of material were generally the result of the explicit demands of the state, rather than of any personal decision. There has been much recent controversy about the extent to which Soviet composers genuinely supported the musical principles they publicly espoused; this controversy was fuelled by the debate over the authenticity of *Testimony*, the so-called memoirs of Shostakovich.

Soviet Russia is clearly a specialized example, but the way in which events find their echoes in music has been acknowledged by a wide variety of composers. Schumann, for example, wrote that:

> Anything that happens in the world affects me, politics, for example, literature, people; and I reflect about all these things in my own way – and these reflections then seek to find an outlet in music.[13]

Schoenberg took a similar view:

> It has always been my belief that a composer speaking of his own problems speaks at once of the problems of mankind. But he does it in a symbolical way . . . expressing matters of philosophy, economy or problems of labour, society or morals.[14]

Tippett, interestingly, was not content merely to allow events to be passively reflected in his music. Rather, he consciously sought in the world the missing pieces of his 'jigsaw', of which he only knew the general outline:

> I know that somewhere or other, in books, in pictures, in dreams, in real situations, everything is sooner or later to be found which belongs for all the details of the work, which is, as it were, ordained.[15]

In certain cases, events may be the cause of a composition, without actually inspiring the musical vision that is at its core. This is often the case when music is commissioned for a particular occasion, such as a wedding, funeral or state event. Sometimes, though, the nature of the event itself may actually contribute something to the individuality of the piece: this is certainly the case for Berlioz's *Grande symphonie funèbre et triomphale*. This was composed in response to a commission to mark the tenth anniversary of the July Revolution of 1830, and to commemorate those who had died in Paris during the uprising. The practical difficulties associated with the commission were great: the music had to be performed outdoors, meaning that much of the sound was in danger of being lost, and it had to be performed while marching, restricting the potential forces to wind instruments, as well as creating great potential problems of ensemble. Many composers, faced with these problems and restrictions, would have settled for writing a blandly bombastic piece: there are few musically interesting and innovative pieces for an ensemble of 210 wind instruments! However, Berlioz succeeded in writing a piece that more than matched the dignity of the occasion and the setting, as a letter to his father triumphantly records:

Our stage was Paris, its embankments and its boulevards. And the old know-alls of military music were claiming that I'd never manage to have the *Marche funèbre* performed on the march and that my 210 musicians wouldn't stay together for twenty bars. In the event these experienced prophets were proved wrong. I placed the trumpets and drums in front so that I could give them the beat while walking backwards and (as I had intended from the start) because in the opening bars these instruments play by themselves, they could be heard by the rest of the band. So that not only the *Marche funèbre* but also the *Apothéose* was played six times, on the march, with an ensemble and an effect that were truly extraordinary.[16]

Artistic Experience

Engagement with other works of art, at whatever level it takes place, has always been among the most fertile sources of inspiration for composers. Discounting for the moment the experience of music itself, literature has perhaps been the art form that has contributed most to musical inspiration, both in terms of the quantity and the interest of the works produced. This is in part because of the variety of ways in which literature can inspire music. At the most obvious level, composers may use literary texts as a source for a song or an opera libretto. In a slightly less direct, but still literal fashion, a literary text may provide the subject matter for a piece: as, for example, when a novel or play is used as the basis for a programmatic instrumental work that does not actually set any of the words of the text. At a more complex level, the sentiments aroused by literature, or the techniques used by writers, may provoke composers to compose music whose style or procedures reflect those of the literature.

Composers of dramatic music and songs have often drawn inspiration from the texts they have chosen to set. For example, Gluck regarded his task as being to *follow* the dramatic emotions of *Alceste* when he composed his opera in 1767:

I have not placed any value on novelty, if it did not emerge naturally from the situation and the expression: and there is no rule I would not have felt in duty bound to break in order to achieve the desired effect.[17]

54

Both Debussy and Ravel expressed a desire to set literary texts whose ambitions matched those that they held for their music. Ravel wished to explore new areas of feeling and selected texts accordingly. For example, he noted:

> Les Chansons madécasses seem to me to have a new, dramatic – voire érotique – element which the subject itself of Parny's poems has introduced to them.[18]

Debussy set out his own ideas about what his perfect opera libretto would do, three years before he eventually alighted upon a suitable text in Maeterlinck's Pelléas et Mélisande:

> My ideal is a short libretto with unhampered movement between scenes. I find the three unities irrelevant. The places and characters need to be varied from scene to scene and the characters shouldn't engage in discussions or arguments: as I see it they are controlled by life, by destiny.[19]

If these composers have been influenced by the literary detail in the texts they choose to set, then others have been more concerned to convey the situation, the dramatic substance of the story. Tippett commented in relation to King Priam that 'it is not the words as such which the composer is setting, but the situations', and Mozart's extreme fussiness over libretti – he rejected hundreds – was due to his belief that most librettists spoiled good situations by paying too much attention to versification and elaborate literary conceits: there were 'words or even verses which ruin the composer's entire idea'. The 'idea' is Mozart's musical conception of the situation, born of his unerring dramatic perception. Later composers have shared his preoccupation. 'What music must have above all', wrote Saint-Saëns, 'is emotions and passions, laid bare or set in action by what we term the situation.' The stimulus of a basic situation on which an opera is based is powerful enough to see the composer through the entire work. Verdi declared that 'I should compose with utter confidence a subject that set my blood going, even though it were condemned by all other artists as antimusical.' Richard Strauss was particularly sensitive to the musical possibilities of a libretto:

> When I first saw Hofmannsthal's inspired play [*Elektra*] . . . I immediately recognized, of course, what a magnificent operatic libretto it might be . . . and, just as previously with *Salome*, I appreciated the tremendous increase in musical tension to the very end.[20]

Even when composers do not set a text directly, they may still be profoundly influenced by the literary works they use as a source. The mid-nineteenth century perhaps marked the zenith of this musical fascination with literature. Mendelssohn was inspired by the play when writing his incidental music for *A Midsummer Night's Dream*:

> I call it great luck to have had such a subject to inspire me . . . What I could do as a composer I could do before writing the overture, but I had not yet before my imagination such a subject as that. That was indeed an inspiration.[21]

Liszt searched, when composing his tone-poems, for musical means of expressing the new psychological areas that were explored by the texts he used as his sources:

> To enrich the form [of a piece], to enlarge it and make it

serviceable, is granted . . . precisely to those who make use
of it only as one of the means of expression as one of the
languages which they employ in accordance with the dictates of the ideas to be expressed. Is music unsuited to cause
such natures [epic heroes such as Faust, Cain, Manfred] to
speak its language? . . . could music do this in the drama?
Scarcely . . . The interest which they [heroes' passions]
arouse attaches itself far more to inner events than to
actions related to the outer world.[22]

No composer's engagement with poetry was more dramatic
than that of Berlioz, whose first encounter with Shakespeare,
when he watched his future wife playing the part of Ophelia
in *Hamlet*, was famously described:

> Shakespeare, coming upon me unawares, struck me like a
> thunderbolt. The lightning flash of that discovery revealed
> to me at a stroke the whole heaven of art, illuminating it
> to its remotest corners. I recognized the meaning of grandeur,
> beauty, dramatic truth, and I could measure . . . the pitiful
> narrowness of our own worn-out academic, cloistered tradi-
> tions of poetry. I saw, I understood, I felt . . . that I was
> alive and that I must arise and walk.[23]

Berlioz's Shakespearean ecstasy provided enough material for
a lifetime's compositional activities. Shakespeare did not only
provide a source, as in *Béatrice et Bénédict*, the opera based
on *Much Ado About Nothing*; he also prompted Berlioz to
experiment with new means of conveying narrative in music,
as in the revolutionary and still unique 'dramatic symphony',
Roméo et Juliette.

Twentieth-century composers, too, have been led by literature into a new world of feeling which they have then sought

to express in their music. Perhaps the most symbolic example of this in the twentieth century was Schoenberg's setting for solo soprano of the line from Stefan George – 'I feel the air from another planet' – in his Second String Quartet. Both the meaning of the text, and the very decision to use a text within a traditionally instrumental form, expressed the desire to colonize new emotional territory. George's poetry seems to have been at least partially responsible for this desire. He wrote the following in his programme note to *Das Buch der hängenden Gärten*:

> With the songs after George, I succeeded in approaching an ideal of form and expression which I had envisaged for years, without having the strength or assurance to realize it. Now, however, I am conscious of having broken through the barriers of a past aesthetic.[24]

Schoenberg had previously acknowledged the influence of another poet, Richard Dehmel, on his development as a composer: he had used Dehmel's poems both directly, as song texts, and indirectly, as the creative starting point for his string sextet, *Verklärte Nacht*. He wrote to Dehmel:

> Your poems have had a decisive influence on my development as a composer. They were what first made me try to find a new tone in the lyrical mood. Or rather, I found it without even looking, simply by reflecting in music what your poems stirred up in me.[25]

If Schoenberg was influenced most of all by the emotional content of the poetry with which he worked, then other twentieth-century composers have drawn inspiration from the structural and technical aspects of poetry. Stravinsky found the formal and rhythmic elements of Russian folk poetry a tremendous stimulus for *Les Noces*:

> What fascinated me in this verse was the sequence of the words and syllables, and the cadence they create, which produces an effect on one's sensibility very closely akin to that of music.[26]

Even in a non-vocal work, he found stimulus in both the formal and spiritual elements of poetry:

> The spirit and form of my *Duo Concertante* were determined by my love of the pastoral poets of antiquity, their scholastic art and technique . . . a musical parallel to the old pastoral poetry.[27]

It was not that Stravinsky engaged with the meaning of the poetry so much as that he responded to its formal, technical qualities. The music was not intended to carry the meaning of the text, but to transcribe its poetic effect into music.

This process was taken one stage further by Boulez in his settings of Mallarmé in *Pli selon pli*: here the composer does not merely assert that factors other than meaning are the most important features of the texts he sets; he also chooses to set texts which themselves question the transparency of meaning. Mallarmé himself regarded meaning as subordinate to the 'musical' qualities of the text: the resonances of the words themselves, the effect of their juxtaposition, the syntactical construction, the poetic forms used. This makes them at once particularly appropriate for musical setting, and particularly difficult to set in an orthodox fashion, since the traditional ideals for which the song-writer aims – allowing the text to be immediately heard and 'understood' –

are irrelevant. Boulez responds effectively to this unusual situation:

> As to the actual understanding of the poem in its musical transposition: how far can one cling to this? . . . My idea is not to be restricted to immediate understanding, which is only one of the forms (the least rich, perhaps?) of the transmutation of the poem . . . A concert piece, based mainly on poetic thought, cannot be confused with a stage work: this demands a maximum of direct understanding in order to follow the action, the events, on to which, if necessary, poetic thought may be grafted. In my transposition or transmutation of Mallarmé, I take for granted that the direct sense of the poem has been acquired by reading it . . . I can therefore play on a variable degree of immediate understanding. This play, moreover, is not to be left to chance, but tends to give prominence sometimes to the musical and sometimes to the poetic text.[28]

Boulez's flexibility in relation to the question of conveying the text shows that he has not merely taken the superficial elements of Mallarmé's text as a 'vehicle' for his music: rather, he has responded to the substance of Mallarmé's ideas. As a result, *Pli selon pli* – the constantly 'unfolding' focus of the work is suggested even in the title – remains one of the most interesting post-war engagements between literature and music.

For obvious reasons, the visual arts have only rarely been used as a direct source for music, but they have often acted as a stimulus to inspiration. Composers may be inspired by the work of artists near to themselves in time: Musorgsky's *Pictures from an Exhibition* is an obvious and supreme example, but the collaboration of Stravinsky with artists such as Alexandre Benois when working for Diaghilev's Ballets Russes is also worthy of note. Sometimes, however, composers have drawn greater inspiration from art that is remote from them, either in chronological or cultural terms. Raphael's *Sposalizio* and Andrea Orcagna's frescos, *The Triumph of Death*, provided a creative stimulus for Lizst, while the work of Piero della Francesca was the immediate inspiration of Dallapiccola's *Due Studi* and Gérard Grisey's *L'Icône paradoxale*. Also, Ligeti has drawn inspiration from Magritte (in *Le Grand Macabre*), and Birtwistle from Bruegel's *The Triumph of Time* and Dürer's *Melencolia*. Mendelssohn found a sense of mystery in Venetian art which was a stimulus to creative activity:

I cling to the ancient masters, and study how they worked. Often, after doing so, I feel musically inspired and since I came here I have been busily engaged in composition.[29]

Debussy's interest in Oriental art is demonstrated in piano pieces such as *Poissons d'or* and *Pagodes*, while Stravinsky commented about Japanese art that 'the graphic solution of problems of perspective and space shown by their art incited me to find something analogous in music'. The *Japanese Lyrics* were the result.

I recently received an unusual commission: to compose a work to be played in the annual Good Friday concert of the Musée d'Unterlinden at Colmar (in medieval times a monastic chapel) in front of Grünewald's celebrated *Crucifixion* of 1515, a painting revered in Alsace-Lorraine as an icon and admired by Picasso, Francis Bacon and many others. *Death of Light/Light of Death*, as the piece came to be called, has five movements, each a meditation on one of the personages in the picture, which, of course, stood in reproduction on my desk as I worked. Through the crescendoing intensity of looking at the figures and listening internally to the music which reflected that looking, and looking again with increasingly emotive musical associations, then listening again, to and fro, I became more deeply involved in an artist's work than I have ever been before. I was completely overwhelmed by its power.

If literature and fine art can inspire musical compositions, then so too can music itself: the relationship between musical inspiration and other pieces of music is a complex and fascinating one. Composers may be inspired to write by the work of other composers, or by the raw material of music itself: the sound of an instrument, a particular performer. An encounter with another composer is sometimes a sudden, illuminating experience. Ethel Smyth, for example, described the first occasion on which she heard Brahms's music:

> That day I saw the whole Brahms; other bigger and, to use the language of pedants, more important works of his were to kindle fresh fires later on, but his genius possessed me then and there in a flash. I went home with a definite resolution in my heart.[30]

Bartók, too, was inspired by a single, formative musical experience:

> From stagnation I was aroused as by a lightning stroke by the first performance in Budapest of *Also Sprach Zarathustra*, in 1902. At last there was a new way of composing which seemed to hold the seeds of a new life. At once I threw myself into the study of Strauss's score and began to write again myself.[31]

Later, though, he felt the need to free himself from Strauss's influence, as he began profoundly to absorb the implications of the music of his own country:

> Meanwhile, the magic of Richard Strauss had evaporated. A really thorough study of Liszt's oeuvre . . . revealed to me the true essence of composing.[32]

Other composers have influenced their successors in a more complex, ambiguous fashion. In certain cases, the determination of younger composers to avoid sounding like their predecessors can be so strong, that it amounts to a shaping force in their music almost despite themselves. A letter from Debussy to Ernest Chausson reveals this process in operation, applied most of all in relation to Wagner, whose influence Debussy came to despise, after his earlier adulation:

> I was premature in crying 'success!' over *Pelléas et Mélisande*. After a sleepless night (the bringer of truth) I had to admit it wouldn't do at all. It was like the duet by M. So-and-so, or nobody in particular, and worst of all the ghost of old Klingsor, alias R. Wagner, kept appearing in the corner of a bar, so I've torn the whole thing up. I've started again and am trying to find a recipe for producing more characteristic phrases.[33]

Ligeti and Xenakis have both described a similar, if much less extreme, process in relation to Bartók, himself now an 'old master': Ligeti stated that 'in the early 1950s, I began to feel that I had to go beyond Bartók', while Xenakis admitted that, having been 'in love' with Bartók, 'slowly it dawned on me that I had to be much freer, much more individual'.

Almost all composers are influenced, at least passively, by the other music with which they have come into contact.

Stravinsky, however, is a supreme example of a composer who made a deliberate, self-conscious use of a wide range of music for his own purposes:

> Whatever interests me, whatever I love, I wish to make my own – I am probably describing a rare form of kleptomania.[34]

Stravinsky, according to Robert Craft, listened only to music that was useful to him for the work in hand. Thus when writing *The Rake's Progress* he would play only the records of *Così fan tutte* and would attend performances of operas by only Mozart, Verdi, Rossini and Donizetti. Likewise, Busoni attended performances of Italian opera for the sake of his own operatic creation: 'I think I shall go – that is exactly the kind of food I require.'

Other composers have been influenced by music from outside the Western tradition. The influence of Peruvian music on Messiaen (*Harawi*), and of African and Far Eastern sounds heard in his youth on Boulez, and indeed of Japanese Nō theatre on Britten, is well known. Steve Reich was inspired to write *Drumming* after returning from a stay in Africa, where he had studied African drumming techniques. In my own case the cadences of Vedic chant crept into my music almost unawares from the time when I listened to it during meditation sessions: listening, of course, in a particularly receptive frame of mind. Works such as *Nataraja*, *Flight Elegy* and *Curve with Plateaux* all contain the same haunting contours, associated with this chant.

Composers may also be inspired by the actual sound of a particular instrument or performer. Ligeti recorded his excitement at being asked by a player to provide a companion piece for Brahms's Horn Trio:

As soon as he pronounced the word horn, somewhere inside my head I heard the sound of a horn as if coming from a distant forest in a fairy tale, just as in a poem by Eichendorff . . . When the sound of an instrument or a group of instruments or the human voice finds an echo in me, in the musical idea within me, then I can sit down and compose, otherwise I cannot.[35]

The initial impulse for George Benjamin's *Antara*, too, was a particular timbre: he composed the piece after becoming fascinated with the South American pan-pipe players whom he heard outside the Pompidou Centre in Paris.

For other composers, it is a particular performer and his instrument that provide the crucial inspiration for a given piece: good examples of this are Rostropovich's cello and Benjamin Britten, Mühlfeld's clarinet and Brahms, Vogl's voice and Schubert. Stravinsky described an occasion where an exceptional performer influenced the nature of the piece:

I finished a piano piece with Arthur Rubinstein and his strong, agile, clever fingers in mind . . . the different rhythmic episodes were dictated by the fingers themselves.[36]

Composers may also draw inspiration for future works by hearing their earlier pieces performed: Brian Ferneyhough has referred to the stimulus given by hearing differing performances of his own famously difficult music. The performer's task, too, may involve inspiration and intuition, as Busoni argued: 'What the composer's inspiration *necessarily* loses through notation, his interpreter should restore by his own.'

Finally, a musical genre can excite and stimulate the composer by presenting itself as the ideal vehicle for his thoughts. Mendelssohn describes this process:

I, for my part, feel at this moment the most urgent desire to write an opera, and yet I scarcely have the leisure to commence even any smaller work; but I do believe that if the libretto were to be given me today, the opera would be written by tomorrow, so strong is my impulse towards it.[37]

Mozart's excitement at the idea of an opera is perhaps even more convincing:

I have an inexpressible longing to write another opera . . . For I have only to hear an opera discussed, I have only to sit in a theatre, hear the orchestra tuning their instruments – oh, I am quite beside myself at once.[38]

For some composers, opera itself has even provided the subject matter for their stage works. Heroines who are opera singers include Puccini's Tosca and Janáček's Elina Makropolous. Richard Strauss's last opera, *Capriccio*, was concerned with the question of whether the text or the music of opera was the more significant: the two sides of the argument are symbolized by a writer and a musician who compete for the same woman's hand. It is interesting that Strauss should turn in this final stage work to a question that had preoccupied him throughout his career as an operatic composer.

Autobiography

A composer's own life is the most immediate source on which he can draw for inspiration, and it has been an important stimulus for many. Smetana, for instance, wrote the following about his E minor String Quartet:

I had wanted to give a tone picture of my life . . . That is roughly the aim of this composition which is almost a private one and therefore purposely written for four instruments which, as it were, are to talk to each other in a narrow circle of friends of what has so momentously affected me.[39]

Many other composers, from Beethoven onwards, have viewed the string quartet as the ideal form for a confessional work, in which private rather than public feelings can be expressed. However, they have not always been as open about their intentions as Smetana. Janáček, for example, designed his Second String Quartet, written in 1928, the last year of his life, as an expression of his secret love for Kamila Stösslová:

> Now I've begun to write something nice. Our life will be in it. It will be called 'Love Letters'. I think that it will sound delightful. There have already been so many of those dear adventures of ours, haven't there? They'll be little fires in my soul and they'll set it ablaze with the most beautiful melodies.[40]

The quartet was eventually subtitled *Intimate Letters* – appropriately, since Janáček's love affair was conducted mainly by means of letters. These have been published only in the last few years, since for many years after the composer's death his family conspired to conceal his involvement with Stösslová. A further letter reveals Janáček's fear that his quartet – which was first performed publicly only after the composer's death – might not match the love that inspired it:

> I think that some day I'll send you my manuscript of those *Intimate Letters*. After they've played it to me, so that I know if it's worth something too in terms of music. You

know, often the feeling itself is so powerful and strong that the notes hide under it, they run away. Great love – weak piece! And I'd like to have: great love – great piece![41]

A string quartet composed the previous year – Berg's *Lyric Suite* – reveals an even more remarkable hidden programme. It was believed during Berg's lifetime that he enjoyed a stable and contented marriage, and his widow, Helene, did everything possible to preserve this myth between the composer's death in 1935 and her own in 1976. It was only after her death that the full information came to light not only about the composer's affair with Hanna Fuchs-Robettin, but about the extent to which this affair shaped every aspect of many of the composer's works. In 1977, the Berg scholar George Perle discovered a score of the *Lyric Suite*, annotated and dedicated to Fuchs-Robettin, which reveals the work's hidden programme. The notes derived from the initials of the lovers – H, F, A, B – are used in various ways throughout the work. The numbers 10 and 23 – which Berg regarded as representing Hanna and himself respectively – are used to shape various parts of the work: even metronome markings are chosen because they are multiples of one of these numbers. Most significantly of all, the score reveals that the last movement of the piece (*Largo desolato*) was shaped around a setting of a poem, Stefan George's translation of Baudelaire's 'De profundis'. The annotations show that a full vocal setting of this text was originally conceived: this vocal line was worked into the string parts, then ultimately withdrawn altogether, but the hidden text contributes much to an understanding of the piece. The *Lyric Suite*, like many of Berg's works, represents an extreme in terms of autobiographical motivation: events from the composer's life shape the minutest details of the composition in a manner that cannot conceivably be 'heard', but which is none the less of immense significance to the composer. For composers such as Berg, a complex personal life almost seems an essential component of creativity: he himself wrote that a man with a stable domestic life such as he was believed to enjoy 'might for a time be fulfilled with the joys of motoring, but would never be able to compose *Lulu*'.

Despite what has been discovered in recent years, Berg's psychological motivation for creating a work with such a personal programme remains somewhat obscure. For other composers, however, composition has explicitly been used as a form of self-therapy or confession, as a means of releasing overwhelming emotions which would otherwise be suppressed. These emotions are frequently connected with the torments of love, and examples are numerous. Berlioz described the *Symphonie fantastique* as a 'clever revenge' for the extremes of pain he had suffered during his early love for Harriet Smithson. Wagner's realization that his love for the singer Frau Schröder-Devrient was doomed to failure caused him to turn to music for consolation:

If at last I turned impatiently away [from Schröder-Devrient] . . . so did that double revolt, of man and artist, inevitably take on the form of a yearning for appeasement in a higher nobler element . . . a pure, chaste, virginal, unseizable and unapproachable ideal of love. What could this love-yearning, the noblest thing my heart could feel – what other could it be than a longing for release from the Present, for absorption into an element of endless love, a love denied to earth and reachable through the gates of Death alone. When I reached the sketch and working out of the *Tannhäuser* music, it was in a state of burning exaltation that held my blood and every nerve a fevered throbbing.[42]

Tristan and Isolde, written in the wake of an unfulfilled love affair with Mathilde Wesendonck, was arguably an even greater achievement of self-therapy: the very subject matter of this work was the renunciation and sublimation of earthly desire, a process Wagner felt he had been compelled to undertake in real life.

The pieces discussed above represent occasions where particular aspects of a composer's life have been used as a source of inspiration, but some composers have argued that their entire output draws on their life, in a more generalized fashion. Chávez writes:

> A composer transforms, in terms of music, whatever he absorbs from the outside and whatever he is congenitally; he depicts his present moment in music, so that, in reality, all music is autobiographical . . .[43]

Weber, similarly, declared:

> I can write nothing about my works. Hear them played! In my music you will find myself.[44]

Mahler is often regarded, perhaps too simplistically, as the epitome of the autobiographical composer, but his own words give some justification for this point of view:

> My symphonies exhaust the content of my entire existence. Whoever listens to my music intelligently will see my life transparently revealed.[45]

No composer, however, has argued more elaborately than Wagner that his entire compositional output was the result of his experience. In 'A Communication to my Friends', he gives

a detailed account of his self-identification with the Flying
Dutchman, Tannhäuser, Lohengrin and Siegfried. He argues,
when describing the hesitation experienced when beginning a
work, that the artist needs to choose a subject with which his
own personality is in perfect harmony:

> Only when his choice is made, when this choice was born
> from pure necessity – when thus the artist has found him-
> self again in the subject of his choice, as perfected Man
> finds his true self in Nature – then steps the Art-work into
> life, then first is it a real thing, a self-conditioned and
> immediate entity.[46]

Wagner's own identity was inseparable from his idea of himself as an artist: his own compositional struggles were idealized and themselves made into the subject matter of his work.
For him, the torments of the creative process itself were
perhaps the ultimate source of inspiration.

Inspiration, Technique and the Compositional Process

The moment at which a composer's experience is projected
on his unconscious mind is an archetypal encounter of external
and internal, of 'life' and 'art': this encounter is experienced
in its most concentrated form within the process of composition itself, where the composer's 'innate' inspiration col-
lides with his 'learned' technique. Each of these elements in
the process makes its own demands on the composer, but it
is only if he can satisfy the requirements of both that a truly
profound piece can be created.

As Wilhelm Furtwängler – now remembered only as a conductor, though he considered himself a composer first and

foremost – argued, the ability completely to integrate inspiration and technique was the mark of the truly great composer. Although his judgements on specific works may be disputed, his general argument seems hard to fault:

> The crucial thing in later life is the extent to which the composer's technique is connected to inspiration. If it becomes as high-handed as it does in Strauss, it is capable of a long and comfortable life, but from within it is capable only of a modest renewal. In the later Verdi too (*Falstaff*) there is a great deal of technique, which our soothsayers admire, and if Wagner did not have his poetry, which repeatedly lends wings to the musician in him, he would have deteriorated much sooner in his hugely developed technique. The ideal case is Brahms, and even more so Beethoven, of whom one can say that the inspiration is technique and technique inspiration, where no note is written which cannot also be expressed as pure inspiration.[47]

For many composers, the hard part of their job is not finding the initial idea – inspired or otherwise – for a piece, but harnessing the technical resources necessary to convert the initial vision into the finished work. Hindemith noted that 'to have a lovely thought is nothing so remarkable': the 'inner ringing' of a man or woman in the street might be just as great as that of any composer. The factor that distinguished the true composer was his ability to make use of this initial impulse:

> A composer . . . is always in danger of losing the original vision . . . One of the characteristics of the talent of a creative genius seems to be the ability to retain the keenness of the first vision until its embodiment in the finished piece is achieved.[48]

He compared the original inspiration to a flash of lightning illuminating a vast landscape: though the lightning gives a vivid vision of the *totality*, no detail may be observed, as would be the case in daylight. The difficulty for the composer is to add the details necessary to the finished work while retaining the brilliance of the original conception.

Wagner compared the relationship between initial vision and final art work to that between a dream experienced in deep sleep, of which no concrete evidence remains in the conscious mind, and the 'allegorical' dream characteristic of lighter sleep, which may be remembembered in great detail. The job of the musical composition, like that of the allegorical dream, is to interpret and thus communicate the inmost vision. Schoenberg describes the stages of composition after the initial vision as arduous, sometimes laborious:

> Alas, human creatures, if they be granted a vision, must travel the long path between vision and accomplishment; a hard road where, driven out of Paradise, even geniuses must reap their harvest in the sweat of their brows.[49]

Hindemith, Wagner and Schoenberg each describe an experience of composition where inspiration is felt as an initial impulse: the role of 'technique' is to convert this impulse into musical form. However, this is by no means the only way in which composition may proceed: sometimes technique is relied on in the early stages, leaving inspiration to intervene when the work is under way. Schoenberg himself admitted the necessity of taking this approach at times:

> An artist need not necessarily fail if he has started something to which inspiration has not forced him. Often enough

inspiration intervenes spontaneously and gives its blessing undemanded.[50]

Ravel described a particular occasion on which 'technique' came before inspiration:

> In 1924, when I first took in hand the Sonata for Violin and Piano . . . I had already determined its somewhat unusual form, the manner of writing for the instruments, and even the character of the themes for each of the three movements, before 'inspiration' had begun to prompt a single one of these themes. And I do not think that I chose the shortest way.[51]

Schumann advises a pupil that it is often necessary to take this route:

> Persevere with composing mentally . . . and keep on twisting and turning the principal melodies about in your head until you can say to yourself, 'Now they will do!' To hit upon the right thing all in a moment . . . does not happen every day.[52]

It is interesting to note that this approach is frequently taken by those composers whom we would imagine to be most reliant on the guidance of instinct and inspiration, those we associate with a 'romantic' image of creativity. Tchaikovsky, for example, acknowledges that a composer must sometimes begin a work without the benefit of inspiration, if for example he has to fulfil a commission. He noted in his diary for 31 July 1884 that he had 'worked, without any inspiration, but successfully', and elsewhere describes inspiration as 'a guest who does not care to visit those who are indolent'. He cautions that even the strongest emotions cannot be satisfactorily expressed when one is in their grip:

> Those who imagine that a creative artist can . . . express his feelings at the moment when he is moved make the greatest mistake. Emotions, sad or joyful, can only be expressed retrospectively.[53]

Berlioz – another artist whom we imagine working at a constant fever pitch – expresses a similar view, writing in relation to *Les Troyens* that:

> Another danger that besets me in composing the music for this drama is the fact that the feelings I am called upon to express are inclined to move one too deeply. This can bring the whole matter to nought. Passionate subjects must be dealt with in cold blood.[54]

Richard Strauss, too, emphasizes the importance of cool, calculating technique, even – perhaps particularly – when dealing with music that concerns high emotions:

> I work very coolly, without agitation, without emotion, even. One has to be thoroughly master of oneself to regulate that changing, moving, flowing chessboard orchestration. The head that composed *Tristan* must have been cold as marble.[55]

As these examples show, a disciplined composer frequently makes use of technique – the external part of his work, where he draws on his professional experience – in order to encourage the arrival of inspiration. Many have concentrated on this conscious aspect of their work, the side that they can develop through diligence, leaving the unconscious to take care of itself. Ralph Vaughan Williams admitted that 'a composer . . . sometimes cannot tell whether he is inspired or whether he is doing mere routine work', while Elisabeth Lutyens argued that 'Sanity lies in applying the conscious mind objectively and allowing the "unconscious" – "inspiration", "soul", "spirit" – to look after itself.' Ned Rorem, likewise, claimed that

> Inspiration, as such, is no special concern of the composer. There is nothing much he can do about it anyway. He takes it for granted and goes on from there. However, he can do something about the tailoring of his technical resources. If his craft is not ready to construct a suitable lodging for the eventual visit of Inspiration, Inspiration will turn around and leave.[56]

For such composers, it is clear that technical work on the craft of composition acts as a specialized form of what has been called 'experience' in this chapter: a stimulus on which the unconscious mind will draw to produce inspiration. Naturally enough, many have found that if such technical work is carried out with thoroughness and insight, inspiration is much more likely to provide assistance. Stravinsky is a pre-eminent advocate of this point of view, arguing that 'Inspiration is found as a driving force in every kind of human activity. But that force is only brought into action by an effort, and that effort is work.' He developed this argument further in his *Poetics of Music*:

> Inspiration is in no way a prescribed condition of the creative act, but rather a manifestation, that is chronologically second . . . Everything is balance and calculation through which the breath of the speculative spirit blows. It

is only afterwards that the emotive disturbance which is at the root of inspiration may arise.[57]

Many will feel that this argument is excessively prescriptive: the examples discussed here are sufficient proof that the relationship between 'calculation' and 'inspiration' can function in many different ways. However, Stravinsky's argument that inspiration can be 'chronologically second' is a useful corrective to the clichéd view that artistic creation always proceeds from a single, unprepared flash of insight. On the contrary, experience of the compositional process itself, like the other types of experience discussed here, can act as a powerful stimulus to the unconscious. The more profound and varied such experience, the more likely it is that unconscious inspiration will assist the composer.

THREE

The Composer
and the Audience

———

I can see nothing wrong . . . with offering to my fellow men
music that may inspire them or comfort them, touch them
or entertain them, even educate them, directly and with
intention. On the contrary, it is the composer's duty,
as a member of society, to speak to or for his fellow
human beings.

BRITTEN

Thus far the individual figure of the composer has been firmly at the centre of the picture. Whether considering the internal workings of the creative psyche, or the range of external experiences that condition and alter the compositional process, the focus has been the same: the composer as an individual, implicitly solitary, creator. Composers, however, do not work in a vacuum: their music is, with certain rare exceptions, written to be heard, and the processes of performing and reception that this entails are themselves influences on composition.

Composers, of course, often require a sense of self-containment, solitude, even isolation in order to create; but many can thrive only when they also perceive a sense of connection to an audience who will receive their work. Britten's speech, 'On Winning the First Aspen Award', from which the epigraph to this chapter is taken, is essentially a celebration of the contribution of the audience to musical creation. Britten claims that, for each piece he writes, he takes careful consideration of who is going to perform it, where it is going to be performed, and who is likely to hear it. The performer and the listener are not simply a necessary inconvenience for Britten, as they have seemed to be for other composers; rather, they occupy a central place in the musical process. For

Britten, music is best when it is firmly located in its own particular time and place, rather than being composed for a hypothetical and anonymous posterity. This does not mean that the music cannot communicate to anyone beyond the audience who first hears it – such a parochial view would have been strange, coming from Britten at the height of his international success – simply that it communicates best when it is 'rooted' in its own circumstances of origin.

Britten's speech is one of the most cogent and committed statements of this case, but his belief in the importance of the audience has been shared by many other composers. Vaughan Williams, for example, argued that the very act of creation was meaningless if no audience was envisaged:

> [It is a fallacy] that the artist invents for himself alone. No man lives or moves or could do so, even if he wanted to, for himself alone. The actual process of artistic invention, whether it be by voice, verse, or brush, presupposes an audience.[1]

Vaughan Williams's statement, like Britten's, suggests a belief that man draws his identity from his place in society: he works for the benefit of others, not just himself. Such an altruistic desire to share the fruits of artistic creativity has been displayed by many composers. Schumann, for example, declares his belief that if one receives a gift from above, 'it is your duty to share it with others'. Hindemith argues that to share the gift of music is a pleasure as well as a duty for the composer: 'This gift will not be like the alms passed on to the beggar; it will be the sharing of a man's every possession with his friend.' Stravinsky, too, describes sharing as both a need and a pleasure:

How are we to keep from succumbing to the irresistible need of sharing with our fellow men that joy we feel when we see come to light something that has taken form through our own action?[2]

A belief in the idea of musical communication underlies all these opinions, since if music does not 'speak' to other people, it cannot genuinely be shared. For Musorgsky, this idea was central: he declared unequivocally that 'Art is a means of communicating with people, not an aim in itself.' Other composers have placed less direct emphasis on communication, but understand none the less that it will 'speak' to an audience. Ligeti, for example, stated that 'I write music for myself but it is bound to convey something to others', while Copland suggests that communication is always an aim for the composer, albeit one that is often hidden:

Whatever [composers] tell you . . . it is safe to assume that although a conscious desire for communication may not be in the forefront of their minds, every move towards logic and coherence in composing is in fact a move towards communication.[3]

If music is communication, then the identity and nature of the second party involved in the communicative process – the audience – is crucial. Like many of the apparently straight-forward terms used in this book, the word 'audience' is more ambiguous and elusive than it would at first seem. At its most banal level, an audience is a group of people who happen to listen to a particular work. (Even this meaning may be questioned: all the composers discussed here have aimed to write music that would serve for more than a particular occasion, so is the audience for the piece merely the first one, or is it the amalgamation of the many audiences who have heard the work, some centuries later?) The problem becomes compounded when we begin to distinguish between the actual audience that physically hears the piece, and the ideal audience – a single person, the whole of humanity, or anything in between – the composer imagines. With which of these 'audiences' can the composer be said to 'communicate'?

Pleasing the Crowd

The need to impress an audience is often a characteristic of the young composer, who may not yet be fully confident of the intrinsic worth of his creations. This desire to impress is comparable, in psychological terms, to the child's need for praise from adults, and it may be that composers who were precocious musicians as children have retained this need, at least into early adulthood. Stravinsky suggests that the desire to be praised was, at least in part, responsible for his musical creativity: he tells how, before he could speak, he won praise for singing a song he'd heard in the country, though he adds that 'Whether my career should be attributed entirely to the early realization that love and praise can be won through a display of musical talent is another matter.'

Mozart, the most famous prodigy of all, remained dependent on a favourable response from his audiences well into adult life, to a perhaps surprising degree. He felt insecure and incompetent when dealing with worldly matters, and his one source of security was his dazzling genius. His constant desire was to impress and astonish – he felt that if he could do this all would be well – and it was this desire, in part, that stimulated him. For example, he wrote *Die Entführung* to impress the Grand Duke of Russia, who was shortly coming to Vienna and who would be delighted to hear that Mozart had written this opera especially, and in such a short time:

> The circumstances connected with the date of performance
> and, in general, all my other prospects stimulate me to such
> a degree that I rush to my desk with the greatest eagerness
> and remain seated there with the greatest delight.[4]

The sound of applause runs jubilantly through his letters, and
such comments as 'indeed I should dearly love to show what
I can do in an Italian opera' show his need to be acknowledged for his talents. It is perhaps paradoxical that such a
profound man should have felt himself under the world
rather than above it.

He was not alone in this, however. Weber, too, had an
'over-anxious regard for public opinion': according to his son
it was 'one of his tenderest points'. Letters to his wife are full
of 'brilliant success', kings being 'deeply moved', unending
applause. Beethoven, associated in later life with an attitude
of 'autonomy', of caring little what the world thought, wrote
to his youngest brother in 1796 that 'My art is winning me
friends and renown, and what more do I want? And this time
I shall make a good deal of money.' Such an attitude is not
confined to the young, aspiring composer, however. Even a
composer as well established as Haydn was when he visited
London in the 1790s could still be influenced by the need to
win public acclaim, as his account of the reasons for writing
the 'Surprise' Symphony shows:

> I was interested in surprising the public with something
> new, and in making a brilliant debut, so that my student
> Pleyel, who was at that time [1792] engaged by an orches-
> tra in London and whose concerts had opened a week
> before mine, should not outdo me. The first *Allegro* of my

symphony had already met with countless 'bravos', but the enthusiasm reached its highest peak at the *Andante* with the drum stroke. 'Encore! Encore!' sounded in every throat, and Pleyel himself complimented me on the idea.[5]

The search by composers to impress their audiences often takes the form of choosing particular genres, styles or methods which are known to guarantee popular success: a process of 'supply and demand'. Mozart, for example, writes that he is using plenty of recitatives in his operas 'for recitatives are now very popular'. Haydn wrote that his late flowering as a composer of oratorio was motivated in part by public acclaim: 'The general and undeserved success of my *Creation* so inspired my sixty-nine-year-old soul that I have dared to compose yet another one, *The Seasons.*' Even Wagner, associated (like Beethoven) with the idea of creative autonomy, was highly aware of the vagaries of popular taste, at least in his early years, as he frankly admits:

Such lightly won success [of some incidental music composed in 1835] much fortified my views that, in order to please, one must not too scrupulously choose one's means. In this sense I continued the composition of my *Liebesverbot*, and took no care whatever to avoid the echoes of the French and Italian stages.[6]

With more mature composers, the search to please their public often takes the form of an acutely refined technique, honed in response to an awareness of what the musical public enjoys. This is found particularly among composers of music for the theatre. Verdi, for example, was aware that his public needed constantly to be excited during an opera, whatever his own inclination: 'I would be willing to set even a newspaper or a letter, etc., to music, but in the theatre the public will stand for anything except boredom.' Richard Strauss, too, was highly professional in his ability to manipulate his audience's reactions to his stage works. His correspondence with Hofmannsthal constantly discusses 'the effect' that particular devices will have on the audience. This statement of what makes 'an effective ending in opera' is typical:

> A crowded stage and big ensembles make bad 'curtains' . . . a solo or a love duet, ending either with a jubilant *fortissimo* or with a poetical 'dying fall', *pianissimo*, gives the best results.[7]

Honegger advocates putting himself in the listener's shoes, in order to work out what will please him:

> When an unforeseen obstacle stops me . . . I sit down in the listener's chair and say to myself: 'After having heard what goes before, what would I wish for which could give me, if not the shiver of genius, at least the impression of success? What, logically, ought to happen to satisfy me?' Bit by bit, following this method, my score is completed.[8]

This process of 'impersonating the audience' may be seen as a model for the effect of the public on the composer: even if other composers do not literally follow Honegger's example, they are effectively engaging in the same process whenever they compose a passage with the deliberate intention of impressing or pleasing their audience.

There are often material incentives to please an audience, of course: those composers who succeed in drawing large audiences to see their works or who sell large numbers of recordings will enjoy financial as well as artistic rewards.

Much has been written about the temptation this places on artists to 'sell out' or, more recently, to 'dumb down': there is a popular image of an artist as an unworldly figure forced to choose between artistic integrity and material survival. To some extent this portrayal is accurate, but it is worth noting that composers have written of the benefits as well as the drawbacks of having to 'sell' their work to an audience. Charles Ives was in one sense a very unworldly composer, in that much of his work remained unperformed and unappreciated throughout his life, yet even he wrote that musical ideals did not justify real material hardship:

> If a man has, say, a certain ideal he's aiming at in his art, and has a wife and children whom he can't support (as his art products won't sell enough unless he lowers them to a more commercial basis), should he let his family starve and keep his ideals? No, I say – for if he did, his 'art' would be dishonestly weakened, [and] his ideals would be but vanity.[9]

Ives seems to suggest that a composer can benefit in terms of self-awareness from the need to interest an audience in his work. A similar view was taken by C. P. E. Bach, who worked in a period when composers needed to compose music that would please wealthy and often demanding patrons, in order to become financially secure:

> Having been obliged to compose most of my works for particular individuals and for the public, I have been placed under more restraint in those works than in the few pieces I have written for my own pleasure. Indeed, sometimes I have been compelled to follow very ludicrous instructions; still, it is possible that those far from agreeable suggestions

may have inspired my creative imagination with a variety of ideas that otherwise probably would never have occurred to me.[10]

For C. P. E. Bach, too, even an imperfect audience was capable of contributing something of value to the creative process.

It would be wrong, therefore, to present the act of 'pleasing an audience' as necessarily superficial or cynical. While some composers undoubtedly have compromised artistic integrity in a self-interested pursuit of popular success, others have displayed a genuinely altruistic desire to give pleasure to their public. For such composers, this desire is the basis of, not a threat to, their musical integrity. Gluck, for example, believed that the popular success his operas had enjoyed in Vienna was a proof of the correctness of his approach:

> My maxims have been vindicated by success, and the universal approval expressed in such an enlightened city has convinced me that simplicity, truth, and lack of affectation are the sole principles of beauty in all artistic creations.[11]

The belief that music's principal purpose is to provide pleasure to its listeners has had a distinguished heritage: from Mozart – who argued that 'music must please the hearer' – to Messiaen, who wrote that 'It is a glittering music we seek, giving to the aural sense voluptuously refined pleasures.' Haydn found inspiration in the thought that his music might provide pleasure to others:

> A secret voice whispered to me: 'There are so few happy and contented people here below: grief and sorrow are always their lot: perhaps your labours will one day be a source from which the care-worn, or the man burdened

with affairs, can derive a few moments' rest and refreshment.' This was a powerful motive to press onwards.[12]

Beethoven drew comfort from similar thoughts:

> From my earliest childhood my zeal to serve our poor suffering humanity in any way whatsoever by means of my art had made no compromise with any lower motive: (except) the feeling of inward happiness which always attends such actions.[13]

For some composers, a profound belief in the need for their music to give pleasure to audiences in their own time and place has influenced their musical style, causing them to turn away from an excessively complex or intellectual approach which might alienate the listener. Hindemith, for example, constantly pleaded against difficult music which drives away cultured people 'who simply are not always in the mood to solve intricate musical problems'. Copland, too, had something of the missionary in him. After writing a series of 'difficult', 'European' works, he turned towards a simpler, 'American' style for pieces such as *Rodeo* and *Billy the Kid*:

> It seemed to me that we composers were in danger of working in a vacuum. Moreover, an entirely new public for music had grown up around the radio and phonograph. It made no sense to ignore them and to continue writing as if they did not exist.[14]

Many composers have found, though, that their priorities have changed as they have grown older. Whereas the desire to please the public is sometimes predominant in the early years of a composer's career, composers are often increasingly

drawn to works that are written mainly for their own satisfaction. Examples of this tendency are numerous. Among
composers whose early inclination to seek public acclaim has
already been noted, we may consider Weber, who believed
that by championing German opera in the last years of his
(admittedly short) life, he was demonstrating real courage: he
wrote that, in *Euryanthe,* 'I have not attempted to fall down
and worship before the spirit of the age.' Wagner's early
servility to public taste has already been mentioned, yet
surely no pieces represent a more determined attempt to overturn conventional operatic taste than *The Ring* and *Parsifal.*
Beethoven's career represents, perhaps more dramatically
than any other, the instinct for autonomy triumphing over the
expectations of the audience. His early taste for public acclaim
has already been noted; by the time of the Ninth Symphony,
by contrast, he could write that 'Here below composing is
only ridiculed, the dwarfs being the all-highest!!!???'

The instinct on the part of a composer to turn away from
a formula that has already yielded public success was well
described by Schumann, in terms that would surely have
incurred the approval of Beethoven:

> The public must sometimes be imposed upon, for it con-
> siders itself the composer's equal as soon as things are
> made too easy for it. But if a composer from time to time
> throws a stone in its way, and even at its head, all will
> simultaneously duck, feel terror, and in the end loudly
> praise him.[15]

Schumann's comment, however, also illustrates the paradox
at work here. A composer may elaborately and defiantly turn
against the taste of the public, and yet if he does it well
enough, the final result will not be obscurity, but still 'louder

praise', as Schumann notes. The dichotomy between the composer's autonomy and his awareness of the audience is not as complete as it first appears. We have said that as a composer becomes older, his attitude sometimes becomes more autonomous: but it would perhaps be more accurate to say that, as time goes on, he increasingly tries to make his audience accept the individuality of what he has to say. Of course, many composers have found that this is not possible with the audiences of their own day. This is why they have often moved away from engagement with the actual, physical audience, towards a dialogue with an imagined, ideal audience – whether that consists of one listener, the whole of humanity or anything in between.

Defining the Audience

Many composers, even those who have proved most successful at capturing the audiences of their own time, have complained about the potentially damaging artistic results of following the audience's wishes too closely. Verdi, for example, displayed a finely tuned sensitivity to the desires of his own audience, yet reacted against his fellow composers' attempts to follow in his footsteps: 'All the works of these young people are the fruit of fear. No one writes with abandon.' For Verdi, perhaps, the coincidence between his own style and the pleasure of his audience was the result of developments made over a long career; younger composers, he felt, were trying to short-circuit the process by pleasing their audiences immediately, with the result that their music became unnatural, forced, constricted.

Like Verdi, Michael Tippett was aware of his audience in the most positive sense of the expression: his career, more than that of almost any other twentieth-century composer, demonstrated a profound sense of social responsibility, and an awareness of the public significance of musical creation. However, for Tippett, too, awareness of an audience did not mean attempting to satisfy its every wish. The essential element of composition was faithfulness to the inner artistic impulse:

> I know of no other absolute in this matter . . . than the power of such creative energies as I possess. My passion is to project into our mean world music which is rich and generous.[16]

This generosity is reflected in the large proportion of his works that fairly teems with notes – the Piano Concerto is a prime example. This profusion against a relatively slow tonal background suggests the richness of a fertile spiritual land. To project without knowing where or into what he projects is not to wish to be cut off from the audience: however, it does imply a preference for the ideal over the actual audience.

Tippett and Verdi were both highly aware of the musical public of their own time – and yet equally aware of the dangers of being excessively swayed by the wishes of this public. This ambivalence towards the audience is perhaps shown in its most extreme form in the writings of Schoenberg, who occupies a crucial position in the history of the musical audience, since he is the composer most often blamed by musical conservatives for cutting off twentieth-century music from its natural audiences. Schoenberg is presented in such polemics as being contemptuous of the audience, interested only in the requirements of his own musical structures. His own words, however, reveal a more ambivalent, even contradictory attitude. Some comments made in a letter to Alexander Zemlinsky from 1918 bear out the popular view:

> I have exactly as little [consideration for the listener] as he

has for me. All I know is that he exists, and in so far as he isn't 'indispensable' for acoustic reasons . . . he's only a nuisance.[17]

However, remarks made thirty years later in a letter to Hans Rosbaud reveal a very different attitude:

> There is nothing I long for more intensely (if for anything) than to be taken for a better sort of Tchaikovsky – for heaven's sake: a bit better, but really that's all. Or if anything more, then that people should know my tunes and whistle them.[18]

This contradiction perhaps reveals a weariness on the part of Schoenberg with the role of musical martyr – in his eyes, with being made a scapegoat by an ignorant public for the so-called inaccessibility of modern music in general. Whatever the unpleasantness of this role, however, it nevertheless helped him to be the more daring, to compose with more abandon. He wrote in 1949, in an open letter to those who had congratulated him on his seventy-fifth birthday:

> Somebody had to be [Arnold Schoenberg], and nobody else wanted to, so I took it on myself. Perhaps I too [as well as Beethoven, Wagner and Mahler] had to say things – unpopular things it seems – that had to be said.[19]

Schoenberg clearly felt a sense of historical destiny – a belief that he had to write in a certain way, in order to complete a link in a musical chain – and this sense outweighed any feelings of responsibility to a contemporary audience, even though it might personally have been more pleasant to have satisfied this audience. To some extent, Schoenberg, being able to place his music in a historical perspective, can be seen to have substituted the imaginary audience of the future for the audiences of his own day, which were too easily blinded by the apparent novelty of his music. Like many composers before and since, he wrote for an *ideal* audience, rather than an actual one, refusing to simplify his works merely because he was not easily understood:

> An alert and well-trained mind will demand to be told the more remote matters, the more remote consequences of the simple matters that he has already comprehended . . . [He] refuses to listen to baby-talk and requests strongly to be spoken to in a brief and straightforward language.[20]

Many subsequent composers have shared Schoenberg's realization that only a very small group of people, at best, is likely genuinely to understand their work: they have had to abandon any hope of seeing packed concert halls appreciating their music. This became an increasingly common dilemma for the composer as the twentieth century progressed, but the ways in which composers have reacted to it have varied sharply. Some have taken a frankly specialist point of view, accepting that their music will never enjoy popular acclaim and pursuing the logical consequences of that fact. Milton Babbitt, in an essay provocatively entitled 'Who Cares If You Listen', argued that the serious contemporary composer ought to reap the advantages of working in a rarified, academic context:

> The general public is largely unaware of and uninterested in his music. The majority of performers shun it and resent it. Consequently, the music is little performed, and then primarily at poorly attended concerts before an audience

consisting in the main of fellow professionals. At best, the music would appear to be for, of, and by specialists . . . To assign blame is to imply that this isolation is unnecessary and undesirable. It is my contention that, on the contrary, this condition is not only inevitable, but potentially advantageous for the composer and his music.[21]

Ferneyhough takes a similar view. Asked in interview whether an audience was necessary for his music, he replied that since there was no possibility of his work achieving a mass audience, it would be pointless when composing to think of any 'listener', other than himself or his closest colleagues:

There is little use in imagining some 'ideal listener' when composing, since the sort of mass audience that makes any generalization of that sort useful is hardly a characteristic of any species of contemporary music. There is no such thing as the new music audience, but rather a chaotic mesh of special interests . . . In the last analysis every composer works for himself, since only he can gather and maintain the impetus necessary for the creative act. Otherwise, I suppose one writes for the dozen or so individuals whose personal opinion and esteem have importance.[22]

Other contemporary composers have taken a quite different approach to the dilemma, attempting radically to change the audience's relationship to the musical experience, in the hope that the audience for new music will be reinvigorated and ultimately enlarged. Boulez wrote that each serious artist is guided in his career by a single overriding idea:

In my own case that idea has been breaking down the wall – or rather the series of walls – that separate the artist from the public . . . Dividing life into watertight compartments means certain death, as I see it: interpenetration is essential to effectiveness of any kind. We need today to achieve more fluid relations between our various activities, and this means that the watertight compartments in which we have kept chamber music, symphonic music, opera house and concert hall – each with its own equally watertight public – must be broken down if music is to be made free and available to the majority.[23]

For Boulez, it is the traditional *cultural* relationship between listener and music that he wishes to overturn: for Xenakis and Stockhausen, it is the *physical* relationship. Both have condemned the practice of the standard concert hall, as being acoustically unsatisfactory and uninvolving. Stockhausen has developed technology that allows the combination of sounds actually experienced by the listener to be controlled:

Normally, the orchestra is situated at such a distance from most of the audience that the sounds become confusingly mixed . . . I, on the contrary, arrange at what precise point the flute, harp and oboe must converge.[24]

Xenakis has experimented with arranging the players in different ways, to allow the listener to become more involved:

Music can surround us in the same way as the sounds of nature surround us in the forest or at sea. The practice generally observed at concerts, of music coming from one source, is merely one possibility of many.[25]

In some pieces, he asks the performers to move around the listeners when playing:

This solution has another advantage as well: the physical proximity of the instruments makes their sonority much more alive than when you hear them at a distance.[26]

Boulez, Stockhausen and Xenakis share a belief that the way forward for music is to *change* the audience, to encourage the listener to rethink his relationship with the music he experiences.

Babbitt and Ferneyhough on the one hand, and Boulez, Stockhausen and Xenakis on the other, represent extreme reactions to a common dilemma: the tiny potential audience for serious new music. Most composers, faced with this problem, have adopted a solution somewhere in between these two extremes: they have accepted that their music will not achieve mass popularity, at least not in the short term, but they continue to believe that it is useful to imagine some sort of listener for their work. Elliott Carter's response is typical:

> As a serious composer, one has to write for a kind of intelligent and knowledgeable listener one seldom comes across in any number . . . And while the listener ideally should be as 'good' as the composer, the composer himself, *if* he is to achieve his desired communication, must in every case be his own first ideal *listener*.[27]

Carter's invocation of an 'ideal listener' recalls the approach taken by earlier composers, faced with a lack of comprehension from their contemporaries: music is self-consciously addressed to an intelligent élite, rather than to the public at large. Mozart composed certain works for 'a small circle of music-lovers and connoisseurs', while Stravinsky wrote that his *Symphonies of Wind Instruments* were intended for 'those in whom a purely musical receptivity outweighed the desire to satisfy emotional cravings'.

Mahler wrote that a satisfactory audience for his work could be found only in the imagination: 'To be understood and esteemed by men of like mind, even if I were never to find them (and indeed they are only to be found outside space and time), has always been the goal I have striven for.' Wagner, too, came increasingly to address his works to an ideal audience which he conceived as an imaginary, almost metaphysical phenomenon. He wrote near the end of his life that 'The less [the artist] thinks of [the public], and devotes himself entirely to his own work, [so] from the depths of his own soul there will arise for him an Ideal Public.'

The notion of the 'ideal audience', evident in these comments, has acted as an inspiration to numerous other composers, though it has often been expressed in different terms: the 'intelligent élite', the 'emotionally sympathetic and receptive', or simply, and rather sadly, 'posterity'. However it is described, we may assert that the ideal audience has in practice acted as a more powerful source of inspiration for most composers than any physical, contemporary audience. However, closer examination reveals that this ideal audience has been conceptualized in very different ways: some understand it as a single person, some as a nation or race, some as the whole of humanity. Once composers have accepted the replacement of the real audience by an ideal they have postulated, how does this affect their work?

Composing for a Single Person

The process of moving from writing for a general audience towards composing with only a few, specific people in mind, is memorably described by Wagner in 'A Communication to my Friends':

I lost more and more the so-called 'Public' from my view: the judgement of definite, individual human beings usurped, for me, the never to be accurately gauged opinion of the Mass, which hitherto without my own full consciousness had floated before me, in vague outlines, as the object to which I am incited to artistic creativeness, not by ambition, but by the desire to hold communion with my friends and the wish to give them joy.[28]

Wagner demonstrates the advantages of writing for people whom one knows: it is more likely that the composer will meet the audience's desires, since he knows the people for whom he is writing; it is possible to gain a clear, accurate reaction from the audience, however limited it is; and, of course, there is the chance to satisfy the altruistic desire to bring happiness to one's friends! All these motives have influenced the many composers who, at some stages of their career, have written with a single person in mind: an extreme form of the 'ideal audience'.

Of course, economic considerations have often motivated composers to write with a single person in mind: where a patron has supplied the financial resources that enabled a work to be written, composers have often taken close consideration of the wishes of the patron, whether for reasons of gratitude or of pragmatism. The relationship of patronage was clearly more common in the eighteenth century than afterwards, and many composers from this period were influenced in all aspects of their work by the wishes of their patron. The patron's tastes frequently affected the nature of the music: an amusing example of this is found in the particularly interesting cello parts of the 'Prussian' quartets written by Mozart for Frederick William II, King of Prussia and an enthusiastic cellist.

Though the great age of patronage of the arts had passed by the mid-nineteenth century, there are still important examples of works being written with a patron in mind. Tchaikovsky's relationship with Nadezhda von Meck is a particularly interesting and complex example of such a relationship. Mme von Meck provided Tchaikovsky with considerable financial support between 1876 and 1890, when a combination of financial crisis and pressure from her relatives is thought to have prompted her to cut off both the support and the relationship. The relationship was more than an economic one, however. During the thirteen years of their association Tchaikovsky and Mme von Meck exchanged more than twelve hundred letters, and this final letter from Tchaikovsky expresses the importance he attached to his patroness:

> I can say without any exaggeration that you saved me, and that I should probably have gone out of my mind and perished if you had not come to my aid, and not sustained with your friendship, sympathy and material help (at that time it was the anchor that saved me) my utterly spent energy and my aspiration to go forward along my road![29]

Tchaikovsky and Mme von Meck never met however, and on the rare occasions on which social proximity did arise they did not acknowledge one another. Tchaikovsky's biographer, David Brown, suggests that Mme von Meck was frightened of the possible effects of the passion she believed she would feel for the composer if she met him in person; from Tchaikovsky's point of view, we may speculate that he preferred to keep his patroness as an ideal and therefore platonic figure, rather than risking the complications that would inevitably ensue if they met.

Wagner's relationship with King Ludwig of Bavaria is another very important example of patronage, since without the new king's support Wagner would never have been able to build his theatre at Bayreuth or mount *The Ring*. Wagner wrote of Ludwig's influence on his work in extravagant terms:

Thou art the gentle Spring that leaf-bedecked me,
That filled each branch and twig with quickening sap,
Thine was the call that out of darkness becked me,
Set free my powers from chill of Winter's lap.[30]

However, it is possible to be cynical and suggest that Wagner's protestations of gratitude were, at least in part, designed to deflect the attention of Ludwig from the controversial, revolutionary nature of the works he was creating under the king's patronage!

Tippett commented on the problematic nature of working for a patron in the twentieth century.

I have been less sure when a patron has wanted a work of art. I doubt if this can be done at all except in the sense that the composer is given some financial assistance to his life while he writes such a work of art as he may; or simply, that the consumer agrees to consume, or to try to consume, exactly what the producer produces. If the patron . . . has not understood clearly the reality of this situation, the matter can easily be a cause for distress rather than relief.[31]

For Tippett, modern culture does not create conducive conditions for the sort of disinterested, altruistic patronage that Tchaikovsky received from Mme von Meck.

A respected predecessor is another frequent and important

example of the one-person audience, particularly if the predecessor was also the teacher of the composer in question.
Numerous composers have been influenced while working by
the image of a particular older composer. Brahms wrote early
works to impress Schumann, and Rimsky-Korsakov was
similarly influenced by Balakirev. Other composers wrote
primarily to please the older musician: Mozart, for example,
chose D major for one particular symphony especially to
please his father, whose favourite key it was. Berg's relationship with Schoenberg offers a particularly rich example of
the teacher–pupil relationship. Berg's work – as well as his
words – clearly shows his wishes to impress, please and be
loved by the older composer. The Chamber Concerto, which
Berg dedicated to the master on the occasion of his fiftieth
birthday, demonstrates this. In a letter to Schoenberg, Berg
describes the construction of the piece like a good and eager
pupil (even though he was himself a well-established composer of forty by this time), and he continues, 'Yes, let me tell
you, dearest friend, how much friendship and love, and what
a world of humour as well as spiritual relationships have been
confided into these three movements.'

Other composers have been inspired by the thought of a
particularly influential friend. Liszt, for example, wrote to
Marie zu Sayn-Wittgenstein: 'I shall go back to work on your
Elizabeth . . . I want so much to do something for you – and
though I am only good at doing useless things, the thought of
you gives them a price beyond compare.' Chopin wrote that
every stage of his work was inspired by his friend Tytus
Wojcieckowski: 'My thoughts turn to you before every
action: I don't know whether it is because with you I learned
to feel but whenever I write anything, I want to know whether
you like it.' Debussy, too, expressed himself eloquently when
describing the influence of a friend, Vasnier: 'You know when

I work how doubtful I am of myself. I need someone on whom I can count, to give me strength. When something of mine pleased you it gave me strength.' However, we should perhaps be suspicious of taking these noble words at face value, since the composer was engaged in a clandestine affair with Vasnier's wife at the time of writing them!

Wagner's relationship with Liszt is a particularly important example of the effect the thought of one other man may have on a composer. Liszt played many roles in Wagner's life at different times: exemplar, mentor, advocate, performer and eventually father-in-law. For Wagner, the thought of Liszt – whom he regarded as one of the few musicians who understood his work – was a crucial element in his composition. He wrote to Liszt while working on *The Ring*:

> Whenever I have news of you, I am filled with a new desire to commence some large artistic work . . . the music of my *Siegfried* vibrates through all my nerves . . . While I am composing and scoring, I think only of you, how this and the other will please you; I am always dealing with you.[32]

Liszt quite obviously had an enormous effect on Wagner, not only because he understood the Dionysian excitement of Wagner's art but also because he realized at an early stage that it was necessary to respect Wagner's idiosyncrasies, rather than try to change them. Wagner found in Liszt the sort of creative mentor every composer desires: one who, in Wagner's own words, loved him sufficiently 'to make it possible for me . . . to be *myself*'. Wagner's words suggest that he regards Liszt as a crucial figure in his creative life: the symbolic father.

If the 'father' represents the archetypal masculine figure capable of inspiring the composer, then the crucial symbolic feminine figure in the composer's life is the 'muse'. As the etymology of the words suggests, the idea of the muse has always been central to music: the word 'music' is derived from the Greek, meaning 'of the muses', suggesting that it was the art form most associated with the particular inspiration that only a muse could bring. The role of the muse, however, is a complex one. She is both the stimulus of the work and the audience at which it is directed. As the stimulus, she is closely aligned with archetypal woman: she is seen as something far more wonderful and other-worldly than she really is, with the power to awaken the deepest layers of the unconscious and shake the man with inspiration. She must not make a false move or she will be ideal no longer. The greatest muses, like Petrarch's Laura and Dante's Beatrice, have been glimpsed by their adorers perhaps once in a life-time, and consequently retained their ideality untarnished.

Of course, the imagery surrounding the muse is strongly bound up with sexuality, and with the idea of a woman as a passive figure, capable of inspiring art but not of creating it; this in turn implies the assumption that the composer, the active partner in the relationship, is necessarily male. Needless to say, this assumption can no longer go unchallenged. This much is obvious, but it is more interesting to consider the ways in which the idea of the muse might be said to operate when the composer is female, or indeed gay. Is it possible, in these circumstances, for a muse to be male? Peter Pears is an obvious example of a male muse, who not only inspired but was the first performer of much of Britten's most important music. Britten's relationship with Pears was complex and ambiguous – in part because of the deceptions in which they were forced to involve themselves at a time when homosexuality was illegal – but whatever the precise nature of the relationship, it is undeniable that such roles as Peter Grimes and Aschenbach in *Death in Venice* would not have been the same without the inspiration of Pears's voice, acting and personality.

Many other composers have had muses who have actively helped to create the piece, by performing it and therefore affecting the way in which it is received by the musical public. These cases differ from the classic examples of the poetic muse, glimpsed from afar, since for such composers the physical presence of the muse is essential: she becomes the vehicle through which the composer's emotions are expressed. Examples of such a relationship between a male composer and a female performer are numerous: in our own time we may think of Berio and Cathy Berberian, or Stockhausen and Suzanne Stephens and Katinka Pasveer, or in earlier times of Haydn and Frau von Genzinger, Schumann and Clara, Brahms and Clara, Weber and Caroline his wife. Both of these last two acted as imaginary critics in the composer's mind: their imagined favour or displeasure acted to shape the work. Wagner's relationship with Elisabeth Schröder-Devrient may also be placed in this category. Even though it was her singing of the music of others that fired Wagner with devotion, the effect of her voice was an enormously important inspiration for him: 'For many a long year, down even to the present day [1851], I saw, I heard, I felt her near me when the impulse to artistic production seized me.'

If these women acted as muses to the composers through the physical act of performance, then others have inspired music in a much more passive fashion: merely imagining them has been enough for the composer. Chopin is a composer whom one might immediately imagine to be a muse-worshipper; it is an essential component of the image of the Romantic composer. He wrote to one such woman that 'I . . . have my own ideal [woman], which I have served faithfully, though silently, for half a year; of which I dream, to thoughts of which the *Adagio* of my concerto belongs, and which this morning inspired the little waltz I am sending you.' However, composers whom we imagine as rather more pragmatic have also needed a muse. Gluck, for example, confessed to the influence of Madame de Vaines, wife of a French state official, about whom he asked a friend, 'Has she still that beautiful Circassian head? I often see her in my mind's eye, when I am working and do not feel sufficiently inspired; she must contribute greatly to the success of my operas.'

Beethoven is a composer whose relationship to the idea of a muse is ambiguous: there is evidence of the influence of women in his creative life, but this is offset by his fiercely metaphysical, abstract approach to music, and his perceived contempt for 'feminine' emotion. Only one passage in his letters is really relevant, and doubt has been cast on its authenticity. However, it is worth quoting because of its characteristic tendency towards idealization. He wrote to 'Josephine': 'Oh, who can name you - and not feel that however much he could speak about *you* - that would never attain – to *you* – only in music.' The 'you' here is represented as an essence, something idealized, Platonic: an idea of femininity rather than a particular woman. One feels that in Beethoven sexuality reaches an extreme polarity. The masculine themes are more masculine, the feminine more feminine, the degree of the contrast between first and second subjects is hitherto unparalleled. He was a man of unusual feminine sensitivity, easy to hurt, responsive to women, liked by women, a sure sign of femininity in masculinity. This is a well-testamented fact which needs stressing in view of the many stories of his aggressive masculinity.

If Beethoven's relationship to a muse was ambiguous and idealized, then other composers may be seen to have relied more clearly on the inspiration of a particular woman. For such composers, the relationship with the muse assumes an epic quality: it is a motive running throughout their life and their musical output. Janáček's covert, complex relationship with Kamilla Stösslová has already been discussed in the previous chapter. Despite her lack of musical training and the rarity of their actual meetings, he undoubtedly felt that he wrote for her. He wrote of *Katya Kabanova*, for example:

> You know that it's your work. You were that warm atmosphere for me, in which, in my thoughts, you were continually present in all parts of the opera where expressions of love occur. You know, even during that time when we still knew each other so little – I already felt myself linked to you closely.[33]

Mathilde Wesendonck's relationship with Wagner, and in particular, with the composition of *Tristan and Isolde*, represents another famous example of a muse. These lines sent to her by Wagner testify to the way in which he idealized their relationship:

> The anguish
> And the renunciation
> Of Tristan and Isolde
> Their tears, their kisses
> In music's sheer gold
> I lay at thy feet.
> That they may give praise to the angel
> Who has raised me so high.[34]

The relationship between Mahler and his wife Alma was also one of idealization, though in a different way. A consultation between Mahler and Freud in 1910 suggested that Mahler was trying to find in Alma the image of his much loved mother: thus, as Alma herself testified, he wanted to call her 'Marie' (his mother's name), and liked her face when it was careworn and 'stricken'. Mahler's obsession with this Alma–mother image was essential to his creativity, as he acknowledged in a letter to her:

> I have always sat down straightaway at the writing-table whenever I was away from you, and thought only of you. This propensity has always been latent in me. Freud is quite right – you were always for me the light and the central point! The inner light, I mean, which rose over all; and the blissful consciousness of this – now unshadowed and unconfined – raises all my feelings to the infinite.[35]

Ironically, it was perhaps in some ways the very imperfections in the relationship between Mahler and Alma that made her so valuable to him as a muse. The incomplete Tenth Symphony, for example, was drafted around the time at which Mahler discovered Alma's infidelity with the architect Walter Gropius, whom she was to marry after his death. Annotations in the score reveal Mahler's anger, torment (one movement is entitled 'Purgatorio'), and ultimately forgiveness: Alma's name is written over the tender last pages of the score, as a gesture of reconciliation. The ideal muse has been preserved intact, even if the woman herself proved fallible.

No composer's career, however, was shaped by the inspiration of muses in a more dramatic way than that of Berlioz: his *Memoirs* are an extraordinary testimony to this influence. At the age of twelve, as they record, he first saw Estelle, a girl six years his senior:

The moment I beheld her, I was conscious of an electric shock: I loved her. From then on I lived in a daze . . . Time is powerless. No other loves can efface the imprint of this first love.[36]

Later in life, of course, he encountered the Irish actress Harriet Smithson, performing as Ophelia in *Hamlet*: 'the supreme drama of my life'. In a bizarre series of events, he came to marry her five years later, but the marriage was a failure – perhaps largely because Berlioz attempted to marry Ophelia rather than Harriet. In later life he would look back over the wreck of their marriage to that archetypal image which had once inspired the *Symphonie fantastique*. Despite this blow to his romantic ideals, however, the image of his first love remained with him. At the end of his life, he travelled to see the now widowed Estelle, after an absence of forty-nine years. His subsequent letters are reproduced in the *Memoirs*:

Think! For forty-nine years I have loved you. I have gone on loving you ever since I was a child, through all the ravages of a tempestuous life . . . The proof is in the depth of my feelings today; they could never have revived now, in these circumstances, if they had ceased to exist even for a day. How many women have there been who ever inspired such a declaration?[37]

Understandably, Estelle, though grateful for his affection, refused to enter into a romantic relationship. The final pages of the *Memoirs* show how Berlioz coped with this final set-back. Rather than complaining of his luck, he elevated Estelle to the status of a historical, almost legendary figure, who lived primarily in the imagination:

I must be reconciled to her having known me too late, as I am reconciled to not having known Virgil, whom I should have loved, or Gluck or Beethoven – or Shakespeare, who might perhaps have loved me. (The truth is, I am not reconciled.)[38]

Despite this final admission, he declared that he could 'die now without anger or bitterness'. Love of a muse was an ideal that shaped Berlioz's entire life, and which he constantly sought to express in his music.

Composing for a Nation

Composing for a single person, or for a selected élite, involves looking inwards, but most significant composers have also at some point looked outwards, wishing to communicate with a public larger than that which can be contained in a single concert hall. The need to communicate not just with a particular audience, but with humanity in general, is fundamental to the composer: as Copland put it, there is a 'healthy desire in every artist to find his deepest feelings reflected in his fellow man'.

In order to communicate with humanity at large, a process of idealization needs to take place: the composer needs to imagine the inchoate masses as an audience, receptive to what he has to say. For many composers, humanity as a whole has been transformed into this ideal audience; for others, however, it is their own nation they imagine receiving their music. This desire for artistic communion with people one identifies as one's own has taken many forms: composers have sought in their music to reach not only their fellow countrymen, but beyond them to the past of the country, its dead, its traditions, its culture and eventually the earth itself.

Chopin is an exemplary case: he always carried a little silver box of Polish earth with him, and in the same way he valued Polish national music in his exile and tried to gain refreshment from it, declaring that 'I have longed to feel our national music, and to some extent have succeeded in feeling it.' By writing in the once rustic dance forms of the mazurka and the polonaise, he did not merely display the outward signs of his nationality, but attempted to identify himself with Polishness, to commingle with Polish blood and earth.

The idea of Germany was as important to Wagner as the idea of Poland to Chopin: like Chopin, too, Wagner was perhaps most influenced by his homeland when he was in exile from it. He wrote *Tannhäuser* while in exile, and he equated Tannhäuser's longing for the 'redeeming Woman' with his own yearning for his homeland: while composing it, he wrote, 'I lived entirely in the longed-for, now soon to be entered, world of Home.' When he did return, however, the actual Germany he found failed to match up to his idealized image:

> This Home, in its actual reality, could nowise satisfy my longing; thus I felt that a deeper instinct lay behind my impulse, and one that needs must have its source in some other yearning than merely for the modern homeland. As though to get down to its root, I sank myself in the primal element of Home that meets us in the legends of a past which attracts us more warmly as the Present repels us with its hostile chill.[39]

Wagner's immersion in this mythical idea of Germany found its ultimate expression in *The Ring*: the primal, uncorrupted nature of this ideal Germany is reflected in the purity of the E♭ major chords which represent the Rhine at the beginning of the cycle. Germany, for Wagner, was not only his ideal subject matter but also his ideal audience: by his determination to build the Festival Theatre in Bayreuth he did his best to turn that ideal into reality.

For Wagner, the homeland existed primarily as an abstract, timeless concept: the idea of trying to 'express' it by using 'real' native folk melody was entirely alien to him. Many other composers, however, have tried to achieve more direct communication with their fellow countrymen by drawing on various aspects of folk music. This process has sometimes taken the form of direct quotation; at other times the composer has tried, as did Bartók, to immerse himself in its idiom to the extent that he 'is able to forget all about it and use it as his musical mother-tongue'. Smetana, for instance, took this attitude: he was proud of his Czech origins and the fact that his music sounded like Czech folk music in idiom, but actual folk melodies were used only on rare occasions and for particular purposes. Tchaikovsky acknowledged that though he sometimes used Russian tunes deliberately, they often arose almost unconsciously in his compositions:

> As for the Russian element in general in my music, i.e. those elements in the melody and harmony which are related to folk song, this arises because I grew up in the backwoods, from my very earliest childhood soaked up the indescribable beauty of Russian folk music's characteristic traits, because I passionately love the Russian element in all its manifestations – because, in a word, I am *Russian* in the fullest sense of the word.[40]

A more overtly nationalist Russian composer, Rimsky-Korsakov, used folk tunes with greater deliberation: in his opera *Snow Maiden*, for example, he drew heavily from his own collection. However, the Russianness of this work was not confined to the surface use of quotations, as he wrote:

> I had hearkened to the voices of folk creation and of
> nature (viz. birdcalls) and what they had sung and sug-
> gested I made the basis of my creative art . . . My warmth
> towards ancient Russian custom and pagan pantheism,
> which had manifested itself little by little, now blazed forth
> in a bright flame. Immediately on reading it there began to
> come into my mind motives, themes, chord passages, and
> there began to glimmer before me fleetingly at first, but
> more and more clearly later, the words and tone colours
> corresponding to the various moments of the subject.[41]

For Rimsky-Korsakov, knowledge of folk melody was only
the most superficial aspect of his Russianness: his immersion
in his own country worked on him at an unconscious, almost
mystical level, allowing him to write music in which his individual identity was less important than his kinship with the
earth, or more particularly, the motherland.

Nationalism in music – as in every other sphere – has
undoubtedly had its negative aspects: the anti-Semitism of
Wagner is only the most obvious and discussed example of
this. In its most positive manifestation, however, musical
nationalism is not the aggressive assertion of all that is
peculiar to one's own people, but something less extreme: the
use of one's own culture to provide a security, a natural spring-
board into a larger, more universal expression. No composer
within English musical culture has expressed this point of
view more trenchantly than Vaughan Williams:

> Every composer cannot expect to have a worldwide message,
> but he may reasonably expect to have a special message for
> his own people . . . What a composer has to do is find out

the real message he has to convey to the community and say it directly and without equivocation.[42]

Vaughan Williams, essentially, is advocating the same sense of 'rootedness', of connection to a particular audience and musical culture, that Britten espouses in the speech referred to at the beginning of this chapter. Britten himself came to realize the importance of his own musical roots by being detached from them, as he acknowledged in the same lecture:

> I believe in roots, associations, in backgrounds . . . my music now has its roots, in where I live and work. And I only came to realize that in California in 1941.[43]

Both these composers write from within a national musical culture: not out of a desire to exclude other audiences, but because they believe in the need for music to be culturally specific. They address their own nation first, then the rest of mankind afterwards. Other composers, however, have sought to transcend their own nationality: to make the whole of humanity their imagined audience.

Composing for the World

No work epitomizes the desire to communicate with humanity in its entirety better than Beethoven's Ninth Symphony. The finale sets a text by Schiller that Beethoven had been considering for over thirty years before the completion of the symphony, suggesting that its ideals were of great importance to him. The 'Ode to Joy' presents a vision of the whole of humanity joined in joyful union: 'Be embraced, you millions! Here's a kiss for all the world.' The text implies a reaching out, beyond the restricted élite that constitutes the normal audience for poetry and music. Beethoven's setting matches this democratic ideal: if the finale was not literally the first piece to bring 'the masses' on to the stage of the concert hall, then it was certainly the first to do so in such a dramatic and self-consciously significant way. Moreover, the structure and idiom of the piece reflect the democratic, inclusive aspirations of the text: words as well as music, popular styles as well as élitist ones, are included within the embrace of the extended symphonic form. The symphony stands as an emblematic example of composers' attempts to reach out to the world as a whole.

Why, though, do composers feel the need to communicate with 'the masses'? What prompts them to write for such vast audiences? A strong sense that a particular message needs to be communicated has united all the composers who have aspired to compose for 'the world'. Indeed, for some, the ability to convey a message to mankind has been the quality that marks out a significant composer. Chávez defines a great composer as 'one who has many things to teach others, things that were not known before', and Schumann as one who should 'shed light into the very depths of the human heart'. Schoenberg defines him as 'living only in order to deliver a message to mankind': a composer should be judged according to whether he has produced 'something which fills a gap in the knowledge and culture of mankind'.

The message composers have wanted to communicate to the masses may take the form of an emotion, an intellectual or moral truth, or a religious conviction. In practice, however, these categories may not be easily separated: a composer may feel that he has a profound 'message', but may not be easily able to define the sphere in which this message exists. At different periods of musical history, different ways of defining the message – emotional, moral, religious – have been uppermost.

The idea that music's purpose is to convey an emotional message – to move its hearers – is particularly associated with the Romantic period. Berlioz described music as 'the art of moving intelligent men, gifted with special and practised organs, by combinations of tones'. Wagner, too, regarded emotional communication as the essence of music:

> Tone is the immediate utterance of feeling and has its seat within the heart, whence start and whither flow the waves of life-blood. Through the sense of hearing, tone urges forth from the feeling of one heart to the feeling of its fellow.[44]

Likewise, Schoenberg (writing about Mahler) expressed the opinion that 'a work of art can produce no greater effect than when it transmits the emotions which raged in the creator to the listener in such a way that they also rage and storm in him'.

Many composers, of course, have expressed suspicion at the idea that a composer should seek to stir his listeners' emotions through music: they prefer to define their 'message' in cooler, more cerebral terms. However the antithesis this implies between emotion and intellect in music is in many ways a misleading one. Beethoven, when he argued that music should fire one's mind rather than stir one's emotions, was only recommending a different type of emotion. When one's intellect is activated, one is moved: intellectual pleasure is an emotion. Hans Keller's aphorism, that 'intellectual music is emotional music we don't yet understand', suggests that to divide heart and mind in musical experience is false: both faculties inevitably come into play if the music is truly absorbed by the listener.

For many composers, the idea of conveying emotional

experience in music has amounted to a moral imperative: it is not mere self-indulgence, but the true purpose of music. Copland, for example, wrote that:

> Art particularizes and makes actual . . . fluent emotional states. Because it particularizes and because it makes actual it gives meaning to *la condition humaine*. If it gives meaning it necessarily has purpose. I would even add that it has moral purpose.[45]

Many composers have shared Copland's view that music has a moral purpose, and that for this purpose to be fully realized both the intellect and the emotions must be exercised. Hindemith, for example, advocated a view of music he described as Augustinian, after the saint:

> Music has to be converted into moral power. We receive its sounds and forms, but they remain meaningless unless we include them in our own mental activity and use their fermenting quality to turn our souls towards everything noble, superhuman, and ideal.[46]

Boulez argued that Western music could learn from the sense of moral integrity he found in the music of other cultures:

> I was struck in a very violent way by the beauty of the Far Eastern and African works – a beauty so far removed from our culture and so close to my temperament – but I was just as much struck by the conception governing their elaboration. Nothing in them is based on the 'masterpiece', on the closed cycle, on passive contemplation, on purely aesthetic enjoyment. Music is a way of being in the

world, becomes an integral part of existence, is inseparably connected with it; it is an ethical category, no longer
merely an aesthetic one.[47]

A faith in the ethical correctness of what they were doing
has sustained many very different composers, giving them the
strength to complete difficult projects. Elgar, for example,
was spurred on by the belief that the Violin Concerto was
'human and right', that the optimistic philosophy in *The
Apostles* 'may do some good', and that 'great charity (love)
and a *massive* hope in the future' were clearly expressed in
the First Symphony. Tippett, likewise, expressed the conviction that 'If, in the music I write, I can create a world of
sound where some, at least of my generation, can find
refreshment for the inner life, then I am doing my work
properly.' Berio, too, believes that his search for musical
innovation is essentially motivated by an ethical purpose. He
wrote of his research into electronic music:

On to this renewal of material and form – which is concerned with subjects of acoustical research ever more far-
reaching – is added also our spiritual problems, this being
the sign of a renewal of conscience (not only musical) in
the individual.[48]

The language used by Elgar, Tippett and Berio to describe
their aspirations – 'great charity', 'the inner life', 'renewal of
conscience' – can easily be interpreted in religious as well as
secular terms. With many composers, it is difficult to distinguish the purposes they describe as spiritual from those
others might describe as religious. The fusion between the two
was taken to an extreme, perhaps deliberately, by Wagner.
He wrote that his aim was to encourage an atmosphere of

quasi-religious contemplation when his music dramas were performed:

> With all his [listeners'] powers refreshed and readily responsive, the first mystic sound of the unseen orchestra will attune him to that devotional feeling without which no genuine art-impression is so much as possible . . . he will now revel in the easy exercise of a hitherto unknown faculty of Beholding filling him with a new sense of warmth, and kindling a light in which he grows aware of things whereof he never dreamt before.[49]

Wagner's relationship to the language and rituals of Christianity was ambiguous and controversial, but for other composers it was natural and obvious to express their aspirations in religious terms. Haydn, for example, wrote that his purpose was to heighten 'the sacred emotions in the heart of the listener, and to put him in a frame of mind where he is most susceptible to the kindness and Omnipotence of the Creator'. Schubert stated that his aim was 'dissolving [people] to love . . . lifting them up to God'. Messiaen, too, wrote that:

> The first idea that I have wanted to express . . . is the existence of the truths of the Catholic faith . . . That is the first aspect of my work, the most noble, doubtless the most useful, the most valuable, the only one, perhaps, that I will not regret at the hour of my death.[50]

I had a curious and abnormal experience of composing with spiritual purpose out of a kind of perversity, almost against the audience, when seeking inspiration for my own *From Silence* for soprano, instruments and electronics (1988). Massachusetts Institute of Technology Media Lab had invited me to realize a work in their magnificent studios. I felt an oppressive sense of technology at its most aridly materialistic in the general community, and, going against my usual practice of writing to some extent for my audience, I decided I could survive only if I wrote in a starkly contrary direction. I chose mystical texts from a Benedictine convent in England and added texts of my own in similar vein, but with Buddhist undertones. I had no idea what the audience would make of all this, but in fact was rewarded with a strongly positive response. Since then I have always believed in the underlying sense of the sacred present in all human beings.

By contrast, I wanted to align my music completely with the community of the church and its associates in *Passion and Resurrection*, my church opera written for Winchester Cathedral. The work starts with part of the Mass, using the normal plainchant. To arise out of the Mass and transform itself so seamlessly ('do this in remembrance of me' followed by the celebrant priest putting on Caiphas' hat and receiving Judas with his offer of betrayal) is to join a ritual tradition. Mallarmé's ideal for modern drama was that it should be an equivalent to the Mass – similarly ritualistic, similarly symbolic; in my work the audience sings the hymns and responses within the ritual, questioning fundamentally the boundary between observer and participant.

Spiritual content in music, as my own experience and that of others has shown, is certainly not restricted to works with a specific liturgical purpose or religious themes. Numerous composers, otherwise very disparate, have consistently expressed their desire to serve a spiritual purpose, and to send a message to humanity through their music. This desire has, in many cases, been accompanied by a belief in the supreme, almost mystical power of music to bind together humanity: to forge it into a single entity capable of receiving the composer's message. Many composers have believed, like Nietzsche, that music should try to recapture the power of ancient ritual. Delius, for example, wrote that:

> Music is a cry of the soul . . . Performances of a great musical work are for us what the rites and festivals of religion were for the ancients – an initiation into the mysteries of the human soul.[51]

For Nietzsche, the strength of the art he advocated – Dionysian art – was its ability to make the individual feel his kinship with a universal humanity:

> Dionysian art . . . seeks to convince us of the eternal joy of existence . . . We are to perceive how all that comes into being must be ready for a sorrowful end; we are compelled to look into the terrors of individual existence . . . We are really for brief moments Primordial Being itself, and feel its indomitable desire for being and joy in existence . . . In spite of fear and pity, we are the happy living beings, not as individuals, but as the *one* living being, with whose procreative joy we are blended.[52]

Others have seen music's power to communicate with the whole of mankind as a function of the composer's love for humanity – the instinct of Eros, as Freud put it. Weber argued that 'Music is truly love itself . . . and while it is understood at one and the same time by a thousand different people, it contains but one basic truth.' Skryabin, characteristically, described a similar instinct in more extreme and tantric terms:

> I will to live. I love life. I am God. I am nothing. I wish to

be everything. I have engendered that which is opposite to me – time, space, and number. I myself am that which is opposite to me, because I am only that which I engender ... I will to be God ... the world, I am the search for God, because I am only that which I seek.[53]

No composer considered the question of how music could communicate with mankind as a whole more thoroughly than Wagner. For him, music contained the possibility of rising above all the restrictions of individual feeling, and of communicating with what was most basic to mankind. In music, he wrote, 'the will feels *one* forthwith, above all bounds of individuality'. As a dramatist, he sought to concern himself with that which united mankind: 'The Matter of what the Word-Tone poet has to utter is the Purely-human, freed from every shackle of convention.' Although this matter is the content of all his music, Wagner brought it to its conscious representation in Siegfried, a figure who for Wagner epitomized what all humans have in common:

> The real naked Man, in whom I might spy each throbbing of his pulses, each stir within his mighty muscles in uncramped, freest motion: the type of the true human being.[54]

Skryabin and Wagner express the artist's struggle to communicate with the 'essence' of mankind in the most extreme terms; but it is perhaps the career of Beethoven, as I suggested above, that most completely epitomizes this search. Beethoven's existence was almost completely subordinated to his art, through which he tried to communicate: in W. B. Yeats's terms, he chose 'perfection of the work' over 'perfection of the life'. Every observer who visited Beethoven in his maturity noticed two elements in his character – his coarseness and abruptness, and his transcendental idealism. He showed nothing but contempt for the vulgar, coarse 'dwarfs' he saw all round him in Vienna; and yet he postulated, believed in, and wrote for ideal, good and noble people:

> Believe me when I say that my supreme aim is that my art should be welcomed by the noblest and most cultured people. Unfortunately we are dragged down from the supernatural element in art only too rudely into the earthly and human sides of life.[55]

As his mysticism deepened, his imagined audience became more and more abstract, the brotherhood he sought became a projection of an idealized self, and the real people around him seemed increasingly vulgar and unimportant. He became increasingly conscious of the need to search within himself for the 'beautiful divine spark' mentioned in the text of the Ninth Symphony – at the same time as his art became projected outwards to the 'ideal world' to an unprecedented extent. His narrow individuality became increasingly irksome to him: his efforts were directed towards the perfection of his art, to the extent that he had no energies left for himself. It was Beethoven's ability to imagine the whole of humanity as a single, ideal audience that inspired the Ninth Symphony: it was the idea of uniting mankind within a magnificent musical embrace that spurred him on to one of his greatest achievements.

FOUR

The Composer
and the Ideal

———

If, in the music I write, I can create a world of sound
wherein some, at least, of my generation can find
refreshment for the inner life, then I am doing my job
properly. It is a great responsibility: to try to transfigure
the everyday by a touch of the everlasting.

TIPPETT

Music is capable of fascinating those who listen to it on a number of levels. At its most immediate level, it is a uniquely hedonistic experience: considered purely as an aural experience it can be entertaining, diverting, refreshing. Profound pleasure can be gained simply by beginning to listen, without any concern about where the music comes from, how it fits together, what it means. For the initiate, other pleasures are quickly added to these, gained by appreciating details of the piece's lines, harmonic tensions and instrumental combinations: as the piece becomes more familiar, the satisfaction of understanding its formal construction provides an additional element of enjoyment.

Even if it did nothing more than provide such immediate pleasures, music's place in the world would be assured, since even at this level it answers a human need that nothing else can begin to satisfy. For those who take the trouble to listen to it seriously, though, it can provide still more; it is capable of communicating with humanity in the deepest possible way, transforming the normal world by providing a glimpse of another one, just out of reach. Music can communicate the sense of an ideal order, a vision of an existence untouched by the banality and ugliness of everyday life. For the composer, the possibility of such communication is tantalizing: the search to express an ideal through music is perhaps the ultimate source of inspiration.

The belief in music's capacity to speak in such a way has united composers from different centuries, nations and religious beliefs; the aspiration to convey an ideal transcends the historical and cultural differences that determine how that ideal is interpreted. For some, the ideal conveyed through music is intimately connected with their religious faith; for others, it is understood as a purely secular phenomenon. These differences of emphasis are less important than the shared belief that music possesses a unique, mysterious capacity to speak of what lies beyond or beneath the everyday.

This perception of music imposes a weighty responsibility on those who seek to make use of its powers by creating new pieces. Composers have taken this responsibility seriously: they have understood that their music may communicate something more than they themselves can describe. For Stravinsky, 'art is . . . a discovery of reality . . . something entirely new *beyond* what can be called the composer's feelings'; for Schoenberg, citing Schopenhauer with approval, 'the composer reveals the inmost essence of the world and utters the most profound wisdom in a language which reason does not understand'. For Tippett, music's most significant social function has been to speak truths that are too profound to be satisfactorily expressed in words:

Music has always been associated with religious rituals and been a favoured art for expressing certain intuitions of transcendence. That is to say, certain music, to be appreciated as it is, expects a desire and willingness on our part to see reflected in it transcendent elements, unprovable and maybe unknowable analytically, but which infuse the whole work of art. This quality in music has permitted such works as the *St Matthew Passion*, the Ninth Symphony of Beethoven, or *The Ring*.[1]

The works referred to by Tippett all communicate an idea of 'transcendence', of something beyond the everyday world. However, they all also demonstrate a deep internal logic: a sense of order, of unity. Without the ability to create this sense, the composer cannot aspire to express the ideal in music. For many composers, the search for musical logic has been both a necessary first stage to the communication of an ideal order, and a profound source of inspiration in itself.

Order

Although the question of order in music has preoccupied composers throughout history, it has been interpreted in different ways. For some composers, order is primarily a technical issue: they are concerned with the ways in which applying particular restrictions can produce positive results, allowing them to choose from an otherwise chaotic multitude of compositional possibilities, thus producing music that is more disciplined. Others perceive order in terms of mathematical proportions or systems, in keeping with a view that music may be understood in scientific terms. Still others understand order as that which makes music beautiful: they draw analogies with the beauty they find in nature or in visual phenomena, and seek to reproduce this beauty by composing music that is similarly well proportioned.

The first of these approaches has been taken by composers from various periods and cultures who have believed that some sort of technical discipline is a necessary corrective to musical freedom. Stravinsky, for example, declared that 'Strength is born of constraint and dies in freedom.' For him, the deliberate imposition of limitations helped to ensure unity and therefore efficient communication. Paradoxically, once this was achieved, the composer could without further scruples abandon himself to his imagination: 'The more art is controlled, limited, worked over, the more it is free.' This view was shared by the composers of the Second Viennese School, who claimed to find the freedom they sought within the strict disciplines of serialism. Far from finding the restrictions of serialism burdensome, Schoenberg declared that it allowed him to compose 'freely and fantastically as one otherwise does only in one's youth'. Webern, too, felt that serialism was an essential tool for negotiating the chaos of possibilities resulting from the dissolution of tonality: 'Adherence is strict, often burdensome, but it is *salvation*.'

Composers have often worked within self-imposed technical restraints, in order to produce a specific result. Wagner, when composing the Prelude to *Das Rheingold*, used only a single chord to represent the river Rhine and the ideal purity the river represented for him. Ravel – scarcely a composer associated with technical austerity – made use in his most notorious work of a single rhythm and melody repeated over and over again: 'I am particularly desirous that there should be no misunderstanding as to my *Bolero*. It is an experiment in a very special and limited direction.' More recently, the American minimalist composers – Philip Glass, Steve Reich, Terry Riley, John Adams – have used small rhythmic and melodic cells, obsessively repeated. Their intention is to achieve a different way of listening: one in which the listener does not expect dramatic contrasts or an eventful musical 'surface', but becomes attuned instead to listening for small variations over a long period of time. For many composers, the idea of placing deliberate restrictions on their own work is central to their compositional practice: they do so in the belief that it will produce a result that is more satisfying to themselves and more profound for the listener. Busoni, for example, argued that 'It is the distinguishing characteristic of the artist . . . that he sets himself new problems continually and looks for his satisfaction in the solution of them.' Copland, likewise, claimed that 'The artist's discipline is a mature discipline because it is self-imposed, acting as a stimulus to the creative mind.'

Many significant composers seem to have shared the personality trait of relishing the overcoming of difficulty, self-imposed or otherwise. Beethoven, for example, could see positive benefits even when describing a coach accident he had experienced: 'I felt to a certain extent the pleasure I always feel when I have overcome some difficulty successfully.' Significantly, he turned immediately to a consideration of music in the letter in which he described this event. This tendency is represented in perhaps its most extreme form in the character of Stravinsky, who wrote on several occasions that he not only liked but needed the feeling that he was overcoming problems. He wrote in his *Autobiography* that:

> I am by nature always tempted by anything needing prolonged effort, and prone to persist in overcoming difficulties . . . I can experience this feeling of pleasure in the very process of work, and in looking forward to the joy which any find or discovery may bring. And I admit that I am not sorry that this should have been so, because perfect facility would, of necessity, have diminished my eagerness in striving, and the satisfaction of having 'found' would not have been complete.[2]

The same point was reinforced in the *Poetics of Music*:

All creation presupposes at its origin a sort of appetite that is brought on by the foretaste of discovery. This foretaste . . . accompanies the intuitive grasp of an unknown entity already possessed but not yet intelligible, an entity that will not take shape except by the action of a constantly vigilant technique . . . Should my work suddenly be given to me in a perfectly complete form, I should be embarrassed and nonplussed by it, as by a hoax.[3]

Problems to be solved act as a stimulus and challenge to the creative mind, and many composers have deliberately sought them, both for their own sake and because they have equated uncurtailed freedom with unbearable chaos.

The examples discussed so far have demonstrated a largely pragmatic understanding of musical order: it is a question of solving the difficulties presented by a particular piece, technique or style. Many, though, have also been interested in order in a more abstract sense. A fascination with mathematics, number and proportion has characterized many of the most important artists of the twentieth century: figures such as Mondrian, Le Corbusier, Yeats and, in music, Schoenberg and Berg, to mention only those from the early part of the century. There are many examples of Schoenberg's superstitious, almost mystical reverence for numerical relationships. For instance, in his essay 'Brahms the Progressive', he notes the correspondence between the dates of Brahms's birth (1833), of Wagner's death (1883) and of the essay itself (1933), asking, 'Does not the mystic correspondence of the numbers of their dates suggest some mysterious relationship between them?' In later life he became increasingly superstitious about the number thirteen, so much so that he even numbered bar 13 as '12a' in some works. He became convinced that the number thirteen would signify his own death:

at the age of 76 (7 + 6 = 13) he became increasingly fearful of the day of Friday, 13 July. He took to his bed for most of this day, but awoke at 11.45 p.m. and asked the time: at thirteen minutes to midnight (11.47: 1 + 1 + 4 + 7 = 13), he died.

The musical results of this fascination with number can be seen in a work such as *Pierrot lunaire*, which is full of interesting mathematical relationships. The external numbers associated with it were all significant: it was his Op. 21 (a number of particular importance to Schoenberg), and it set twenty-one poems of thirteen lines each. The ensemble consisted of five players playing eight instruments (5 + 8 = 13) and Schoenberg used a different combination for each setting. Internally, too, Schoenberg's music experiments with proportion and symmetry to a degree hitherto unprecedented in his music: 'Der Mondfleck', for example, is both a complete palindrome and a double canon. Schoenberg's fascination with number was shared by his pupil Alban Berg. For the younger composer, 23 was a particularly significant number: he used it in the *Lyric Suite* to govern both the number of bars in a section and the metronome markings, while other numbers were employed to symbolize various characters within its secret narrative.

Schoenberg's thought was developed further after the Second World War in music of extreme mathematical sophistication by Milton Babbitt – every aspect of the music controlled by a unifying 'set' – a set of numbers. That was in America, where Schoenberg had taken refuge from fascism. In Europe the emotional hysteria of Nazism led to a similar response. The cool objectivity of number patterns controlled even such emotionally expressive aspects as dynamics.

If numbers were the foundation of mathematical order in the music of Schoenberg and Berg and their legacy, then for other composers proportion has been all important. Roy

Howat's study of Debussy convincingly argues that he made extensive use of 'golden sections': climaxes of movements and pieces were planned to occur after a certain proportion of the music had taken place, a proportion arrived at through mathematical formulae. If Howat's findings are correct, then they reveal an ability on Debussy's part to view his compositions as abstract, mathematical structures, independent of their manifestation as sound. Debussy seems to have used the 'golden section' principle somewhat furtively, but other composers have made more obvious use of it: for example, Bartók or Xenakis, who encountered the idea when studying architecture with Le Corbusier.

The real significance of these examples is to show that abstract mathematical relationships can be as important to music as the characteristics more readily associated with it: in Schoenberg's words, 'The mental pleasures caused by structural beauty can be tantamount to the pleasure deriving from emotional qualities.' The mention made by Schoenberg of beauty holds the key to this issue: for him, as for many composers, mathematical proportion was valued not only for its own sake but because it held out the possibility of achieving an abstract, pure beauty in music. For a composer who is interested in communicating a vision of an ideal world, the study of mathematics is a logical first step, as John Tavener writes, 'The artist is constantly represented as imitating heavenly forms: therefore the references of symbolic forms must be as precise as mathematics.'

An example given by Stravinsky illustrates this connection between mathematics and a particular form of visual beauty. He discusses the system he used when composing *Movements for Piano and Orchestra*:

The fifth movement, for instance, (which cost me a gigantic

effort, I rewrote it twice), uses a construction of twelve verticals. Five orders are rotated instead of four, with six alternatives for each of the five, while at the same time the six 'work' in all directions, as though through a crystal.[4]

The crystal is an apt metaphor for the effect he wished to achieve in this piece. It is an object that is equally beautiful when viewed from all directions: its effect does not therefore depend on the position of the viewer, and may be said to be objective rather than subjective. It represents a pure beauty, one from which the maker's individuality is entirely absent: Stravinsky's invocation of it here confirms that he is interested in creating a perfect, abstract form, not with expressing emotion or his own personality. As Stravinsky wrote elsewhere, 'All [the composer] knows or cares about is his apprehension of the contour of the form, for the form is everything.'

For Stravinsky, here at least, the musical form is the object of an almost scientific scrutiny: like a scientist, he tries to achieve an entirely objective understanding of the phenomenon, refusing to allow his observations to be coloured by any hint of personal involvement. A quasi-scientific attitude to composition has been displayed by many other twentieth-century composers, who have argued that scientific knowledge can be drawn on for assistance when planning musical structures. Varèse wrote that 'There is solidarity between scientific development and the progress of music. Throwing new light on nature, science permits music to progress – or rather to grow and change with changing times – by revealing to our senses harmonies and sensations before unfelt.' Xenakis, similarly, stated that 'I became convinced . . . that one can achieve universality, not through religion, not through emotions or tradition, but through the sciences.

Through a scientific way of thinking.' George Benjamin has also spoken of the influence of recent scientific developments on his work:

> Form has always been one of my absolute priorities. I have always felt the need to tackle organic concepts in music. Recently reading several books about chaos theory and having studied mathematics and chemistry at school, I have been fascinated by ideas of instability and, above all, the relation between simplicity and complexity. It seems that it was wrong to have separated chaos and order in the past; they are two manifestations of the same, unstable source.[5]

As George Benjamin's account makes explicit, an obsessive concern with formal order often compels the composer to search for a scientific perspective on his work. Some composers have drawn on mathematical and scientific methods of structuring their music in an attempt to create an order in their work that stands up to objective scrutiny. This attempt is perhaps symptomatic of a desire to transcend the vagaries of musical fashion: to compose music that, because of its pure, natural order, will be beautiful for all time, not merely according to the dictates of current beliefs. Many composers have expressed a faith in the possibility of such a beauty: Busoni argued that 'there is an absolute, demonstrable beauty and perfection and there are things that please certain people at certain times and will be looked upon as beautiful by them', while D'Indy suggested that the composer should know 'how to eliminate from the work of art all excessive matter in order to keep only that which is eternal: the balance of the elements of beauty'. For Richard Strauss, this eternal quality was nowhere better represented than in the music of

Mozart. We may infer that the characteristics he seeks to impart to his own music are similar:

> Untrammelled by any mundane Form, the Mozartian melody is the *Ding an sich*. It hovers like Plato's Eros between heaven and earth, between mortality and immortality – set free from 'the Will' – it is the deepest penetration of artistic fancy and of the subconscious into the innermost secrets, into the realm of the 'prototypes'.[6]

The search to create something that is absolute, timeless, is perhaps at the root of the interest in order which we have observed in all the composers discussed. Many would sympathize with Stravinsky's view that music is peculiarly well equipped to create a vision of an ideal order:

> The phenomenon of music is given to us with the sole purpose of establishing an order in things, including, and particularly, the co-ordination between man and time. To be put into practice, its indispensable and single requirement is construction. Construction once completed, this order has been attained, and there is nothing more to be said. It would be futile to look for, or expect anything else from it. It is precisely this construction, this achieved order, which produces in us a unique emotion having nothing in common with our ordinary sensations and our responses to the impressions of daily life.[7]

Stravinsky's remark may be an overstatement, but it is one that explains the great importance that so many composers have attached to the idea of 'order'. This is no superficial issue: the concept of order lies at the heart of composers' beliefs about what their music can do. It is only by achieving this ideal order – apparently mystical to the outsider, but concrete and practical to the composer who seeks it – that music can free itself from the everyday, producing in the listener the 'unique emotion' to which Stravinsky refers.

Unity

The link between unity and order is obvious: music cannot be unified if it is not ordered. Unity, however, implies something more: not only that the elements of the work are logically consistent and connected, but also a more profound sense that each contributes to a single whole, and that the effect of each part is in proportion with and subordinated to the requirements of that whole.

This idea of unity is most immediately associated with the music of the classical era. The mature music of Haydn, and almost all of Mozart, exhibits a new type of order: widely contrasting elements of melody, rhythm and harmony are welded into one law-abiding equilibrium, with such success that we instinctively feel that the disparate elements *belong* together, that they could not be placed anywhere else without great detriment to the effect of the whole. This was a more highly developed and confident notion of unity than that displayed in the baroque period: with some exceptions, baroque composers did not employ such diverse material, so the achievement of synthesis was correspondingly less. The composers of the classical era did not work in a vacuum, however: their new confidence in the idea of unity may easily be related to the new world view brought about by Galileo, Kepler and Newton, the scientists of the Enlightenment who sought to demonstrate the interrelatedness of all physical phenomena.

Later composers have been no less preoccupied with the

ideal of unity. Beethoven, in a conversation reported by Bettina von Arnim to Goethe, stated that 'Music gives the mind a relation to the Harmony. Any single, separate idea has in it the feeling of the Harmony, which is Unity.' This emphasis on unity had clear effects on his compositional practice: he wrote to someone who requested alterations in a piece that 'Once one has thought out a whole work which is based even on a bad text, it is difficult to prevent this whole from being destroyed if individual alterations are made here and there.' We know that he usually sketched movements *in toto*, marking in the essentials of rhythmic motion till he could view the developments and contrasts within it as part of a single entity, like the aspects of an architect's unbuilt building.

This rigorous view of a movement or piece as a single structure has been very influential on later composers. Busoni is one of several composers who uses the metaphor of a seed growing to describe the relationship between a musical idea and the piece it inspires. It is an image that suggests that the composer views a musical structure as organic, with its own life, like a plant or creature:

> Every motive – so it seems to me – contains like a seed, its life-germ within itself . . . in each motive there lies the embryo of its fully developed form; each one must unfold itself differently, yet each obediently follows the law of eternal harmony.[8]

Copland uses a similar metaphor:

> These germinal ideas . . . seem to be begging for their own life, asking their creator, the composer, to find the ideal envelope for them, to evolve a shape and colour and content that will most fully exploit their creative potential.[9]

Stravinsky was also seemingly obsessed by unity, despite the stark juxtaposition of material in many of his pieces which gives a superficial impression of discontinuity: he declared that 'The essential question that occupies the musician . . . always and inevitably reverts back to the pursuit of the One out of the Many.' In later life, he took this question to what seemed to him to be a logical conclusion, arguing that 'construction must replace contrasts' and adopting many of the methods of serialism.

For Stravinsky, serialism increasingly became a way of selecting, ordering and thus unifying his material, and his decision to make use of it is one that was shared by many postwar composers. Those working with electronic music in particular were faced with a baffling plethora of possible sounds, and so it is not surprising that, as Stockhausen writes, 'A few composers have nourished the strong desire to submit radically to a unitary standard principle all the aspects of their compositions.' In its most extreme form, this 'standard principle' was total serialism – a system in which not only pitches, but also durations, dynamics, registers, densities and even timbres and spatial projection were made subject to a strict ordering principle. In Stockhausen's opera cycle *Licht* the principle extends to lighting and staging too. Even as early as 1958 Stockhausen was realizing in *Kontakte* a 'concept of unity in electronic music' which saw as one decelerating sweep of vibration speed the gamut from 13,000 cycles per second to roughly one cycle per hour. The 'domains' of pitch, rhythm and form represented by these frequencies merged into one another as the shapes were radically accelerated or slowed down on tape recorders or in imagination; in Stockhausen's words, 'All of musical time was unified under a common principle.'

The principle of unity was, of course, also central to the approach of the composers of the Second Viennese School, who first developed serial methods of construction. Schoenberg's method was often to start with a single motive, then to view the possibilities and consequences resulting from it: 'The craftsman is proud . . . of the profundity of his ideas and his capacity of penetrating to the most remote consequences of an idea.' This approach was taken even further by Webern, who wrote of his own practice that 'There is this constant effort to derive as much as possible from one principal idea.' In some cases – the Concerto, Op. 24, for example – the principal idea was nothing more than a pair of intervals, from which the row, and the work, were constructed.

For Schoenberg, the ability to work in this way, testing ideas until their logical conclusion was reached, was the mark of the true composer: 'The capacity to fulfil instinctively and unconsciously the demands of constructive lawfulness in music should be considered the natural condition of a talent.' As with the classical composers, however, the emphasis on unity was no mere technical preference: it drew its context from a broader set of philosophical convictions. Schoenberg himself drew a link between his view of music, and a philosopher's view of heaven:

> The unity of musical space demands an absolute and unitary perception. In this space as in Swedenborg's heaven . . . there is no absolute down, no right or left, forward or backward.[10]

For Schoenberg – as for Stravinsky in the quotation discussed on pp. 137–8 – achieving his ideal of unity is a necessary precondition for music to fulfil its true function, of representing the ideal. Music, like heaven, must obey its own laws, not those of the everyday world; and the most fundamental of these laws is that of unity.

Schoenberg, Stockhausen and many others clearly understand the concept of unity in metaphysical as well as practical terms. It does not merely help them to look inwards to their own music, ensuring that it is rigorously and economically constructed; it also encourages them to look outward, to see the fundamental kinship between their music and the world beyond. Busoni, for example, wrote that 'I endeavour to draw upon the Infinite which surrounds mankind and to give it back in created form.' Liszt, too, believed that music could be explained according to the same laws that governed the natural world:

> Art has . . . an existence not determined by man's intention, the successive phases of which follow a course independent of his deciding and predicting. It exists and flowers in various ways in conformity with basic conditions whose inner origin remains just as much hidden as does the force which holds the world in its course.[11]

And Hindemith, noting the similarities between the measurement of music and that of the other sciences, commented that 'This could lead us to the belief that there is some sound foundation in the ancient idea of a universe regulated by musical laws – or, to be more modest, a universe whose laws of construction and operation are complemented by a spiritual reflection in musical organisms.'

For such composers, the idea of unity is not merely an aesthetic preference: it is a moral imperative. Music's own, internal unity is both a necessary ingredient for, and a symbol of, music's ability to bring unity to the world. This was the conclusion drawn by Stravinsky in the *Poetics*; he quotes a Chinese sage's view that 'music is what unifies', and goes on to comment:

The unity of the work has a resonance all its own. Its echo, caught by our soul, sounds nearer and nearer. Thus the consummated work spreads abroad to be communicated and finally flows back towards its source. The cycle, then, is closed. And that is how music comes to reveal itself as a form of communion with our fellow man – and with the Supreme Being.[12]

Aspiring towards the Ideal

An ability to create music that is ordered and unified is clearly an important prerequisite if a composer wishes to communicate a vision of the ideal. However, this ability, on its own, is not enough: if it is not joined to other qualities, the composer will produce music that is formally coherent but sterile. A command of musical structure must be allied to the human qualities of curiosity, restlessness, ambition. A composer must aspire to take his music beyond the mundane, to communicate a grander, more profound vision: he must search for the ideal, both in life and in music.

In a sense, this aspiration on the part of the composer is simply an intensified version of a sensation experienced by many people. As Vaughan Williams wrote:

We all, whether we are artists or not, experience moments when we want to get outside the limitations of ordinary life, when we see dimly a vision of something beyond . . . those whom we call artists find the desire to create beauty irresistible.[13]

The artist, then, is distinguished less by his *desire* for transcendental experience, than by his *ability* to create a beautiful object which goes some way towards satisfying that desire.

His job is to lead the way for his fellow human beings. He is an ambassador for mankind in the world of the ideal, as Hindemith wrote:

> There is a region of visionary irrationality in which the veiled secrets of art dwell, sensed but not understood, implored but not commanded, imparting but not yielding. He cannot enter this region, he can only pray to be elected one of its messengers. If his prayers are granted and he, armed with wisdom and gifted with reverence for the unknowable, is the man whom Heaven has blessed with the genius of creation, we may see in him the donor of the precious present we all long for in the great music of our time.[14]

The artist who wishes to convey such a vision requires many qualities. He needs the determination to persist in his creative journey, despite possible adversity. In Verdi's words:

> The artist must scrutinize the future, see in the chaos new worlds; and if on the new road he sees in the far distance a small light, let him not be frightened of the dark which surrounds him; let him go on and if sometimes he stumbles and falls, let him get up and still press on.[15]

He also needs a clarity of vision that allows him to see beyond the superficial, to the deepest levels of the material with which he deals. Mahler wrote of his desire to know the world in its purest form:

> And I *must* love it, this world with its deception and light-mindedness and eternal laughter. O that some god might tear the veil from before my eyes, so that my clear glance might penetrate to the very dregs of the earth! O, I would

like to gaze upon it, this earth all laid bare without decoration or adornment, as it lay open before its Creator; then I would step before its spirit.[16]

He also needs to be willing to pursue the logic of his own ideas to the furthest possible conclusion. Wagner found that the process of composition itself allowed him to understand the deepest implications of his own work: significances the mere texts of his libretti concealed. He wrote about the composition of *Siegfried* that 'Curiously enough, it is only during composition that the real essence of my poem is revealed to me. Everywhere I discover secrets which had been previously hidden from me, and everything in consequence grows more passionate, more impulsive.'

The visionary qualities required by the composer have been described in many different ways. Several composers have used metaphors of ascension and flight, in order to convey the idea that music gives mankind the ability to rise above everyday life, and into a mysterious area above. Beethoven, for example, declared 'Why, Daedalus, when confined to the labyrinth, invented the wings which lifted him *upwards* and out into the air. Oh I too shall find them, these wings.' Liszt used a metaphor of a ladder to convey a similar sentiment: he spoke of 'that mysterious Jacob's Ladder with which art links heaven and earth', and argued that it was the artist's duty to climb the ladder in order to bring higher things into life on earth. The metaphor of Jacob's Ladder was of great importance to Schoenberg, too. He planned – though, perhaps significantly, never completed – a vast oratorio entitled *Die Jakobsleiter*, a setting of his own libretto concerning the struggle of souls caught in a limbo between death and reincarnation: they are urged onwards by figures including the Archangel Gabriel.

The artist's creative journey towards an ideal vision is often fuelled by personal adversity. The conversion of negative emotions into creative activity has been a common tendency among composers: as Cyril Scott put it, 'The capacity to create something new proceeds from a certain divine discontent.' For many, pain and suffering have actually seemed like a test that had to be undergone, if true artistic achievement was to be experienced. In Beethoven's words:

Man cannot avoid suffering; and *in this respect his strength must stand the test*, that is to say, he must *endure without complaining and feel his worthlessness* and *then again* achieve *his perfection*, that perfection which the Almighty will then bestow upon him.[17]

Schubert, too, saw unhappiness as beneficial to the development of the artist:

Pain sharpens the understanding and strengthens the mind; whereas joy seldom troubles about the former and softens the latter or makes it frivolous.[18]

Pain and suffering experienced in life increase the artist's determination to create an ideal world through his music, as letters from Beethoven show:

Continue to raise yourself higher and higher into the divine realm of art. For there is no more undisturbed, more unalloyed or pure pleasure than that which comes from such an experience . . . For you, poor B, no happiness can come from outside. You must create everything for yourself in your own heart; and only in the world of ideals can you find friends.[19]

In some cases of extreme anguish, musical stimulus has even been drawn from a desire for death. In 1854, after reading Schopenhauer, Wagner wrote to Liszt that 'If even now I feel this hurricane within me, I have at least found a quietus which in wakeful nights helps me to sleep. This is the genuine ardent longing for death, for absolute unconsciousness, total non-existence; freedom from all dreams is our only final salvation.' Such sentiments were by no means the preserve of the committed Schopenhauerean, however, as this poem written by Schubert after a serious attack of illness proves:

> With a holy soul I yearn
> Life in fairer worlds to learn;
> Would this gloomy earth might seem
> Filled with Love's almighty dream . . .
> Take my life, my flesh and blood,
> Plunge it all in Lethe's flood,
> To a purer stronger state
> Deign me, Great One, to translate.[20]

The desire for death, by heightening a fascination with the afterlife, can paradoxically lead to creative stimulus.

The life of an artist who wishes to convey a profound vision, within a society that does not necessarily want to hear it, is unlikely to be easy. Tippett wrote of the way in which the artist's duty in this respect ran against the grain of what society encouraged:

There is no question in our day of the artist receiving a free mandate from *society* to create. The mandate of society is to entertain . . . But the mandate of the artist's own nature . . . is to reach down into the depths of the human psyche and bring forth the tremendous images of things to come. These images are not yet art. It takes a lifetime's work to mould them into works of art. For this the artist can have no reward but in the joy of doing it. He creates, because without art, in this deep and serious sense, the nation dies. His mandate is inescapable.[21]

If the artist receives few rewards within human society, then he is offered some compensation for this by the joyful vision of a better world, which he may experience while composing. Wagner wrote that, when composing *Tannhäuser*, 'I felt myself outside the modern world, and mid a sacred, limpid aether which, in the transport of my solitude, filled me with that delicious awe we drink in upon the summits of the Alps.' Saint-Saëns, similarly, wrote that, when composing, 'One experiences a sort of immense, superhuman happiness; one pities the town from which one comes, the civilization to which one belongs; one no longer wishes to go down amongst men again.' Unfortunately for the composer, such experiences are necessarily temporary. As Beethoven wrote, 'Vulgar humanity only too often drags [the artist] down against his will from those pure ethereal heights.' Mahler described a similar sense of disappointment:

Unfortunately, this wonderful entering-into-possession-of-oneself is undone the moment one returns to the noise and confusion of everyday life. The only thing then is to think oneself back into that blissful state, and to make it a practice at every opportunity to look back at that other world and to draw one breath of that other air.[22]

The composer's aspirations have thus far been described exclusively in metaphysical terms: what, then, are the musical consequences of this yearning to communicate an ideal vision? The impatience with the everyday world of human affairs, which the visionary artist generally feels, is often paralleled by an impatience with the restrictions of the contemporary concert hall. The composer frequently aspires to create a sound, a musical experience, that goes beyond what the technology of his day can provide. Berlioz, for example, concluded his treatise on orchestration by describing an imaginary orchestra, infinitely larger than any that had ever been assembled, and therefore offering infinitely more subtle possibilities of timbral combinations:

> In the thousands of combinations obtainable with the monumental orchestra we have just described would be found a harmonic richness, a truthfulness of timbres, a succession of contrasts that cannot be compared with anything that has been accomplished in art up to the present, and above all an incalculable melodic power, both expressive and rhythmic, a force of penetration unlike any other, a prodigious sensitivity to nuances in the ensemble and in its parts.[23]

Berlioz's frustration with the gap between the sound he aspires to, and the sound the orchestras of his day could actually produce, is palpable. It is a frustration that many later composers would recognize. Debussy, for example, wrote of his dissatisfaction with the stuffy rituals of the concert hall of his day. He wrote of his vision for 'music in the open air':

> Imagine a large orchestra augmented with the sound of the human voice. (No, not a choral society, thank you!) Here would lie the embryo of music especially designed for the

open air: new ideas flowing in broad lines from both the orchestra and voices. It would float from the tops of the trees, through the light of the open air, and any harmonic progression that sounded stifled within the confines of a concert hall would certainly take on a new significance. Perhaps this is the answer to the question of how to rid music of all those petty mannerisms of form and tonality – arbitrary questions with which music is unfortunately encumbered.[24]

Like Berlioz, Debussy dreamed of sounds that were condemned to remain within his imagination. More recently, Stockhausen expressed a comparable frustration at the technological impossibility of realizing his ideas:

This morning, I've spent two hours discussing with the technicians of IRCAM what we'll be able to perform in the course of our next tour. Most of the proposals are unrealizable. It often ends up being impossible to arrange the microphones in the right way. You work, then, with limits so restricted that they make you think of the limitations endured by a superior spirit struggling with the ecology of a planet in formation. Most composers adapt to circumstances, to places, to climate. But, for too long now, art has been functioning as a series of compromises – and for centuries it's lived in docile conformism. I don't want to be a conformist.[25]

Berlioz, Debussy and Stockhausen have each imagined a musical 'world' far beyond what could actually be realized. It is this refusal 'to be a conformist' – this willingness to imagine the impossible – that marks each out as a genuinely visionary composer. Robert Browning wrote that 'A man's reach must exceed his grasp/Or what's a heaven for?': by reaching far beyond what the musicians of their day could grasp, each of these composers made it possible to imagine a musical 'heaven'. It is through the very act of aspiration that it becomes possible for music to communicate an idea of paradise.

Paradise in Music

Music's ability to communicate to mankind an idea of what lies beyond and above everyday life is, for many composers, its most important characteristic. Their belief in this ability has been expressed in many different ways – religious and secular, emotional and intellectual – but we can detect common ground within their perceptions of what makes music unique. Many, whatever their other beliefs, have shared the view of Schumann that 'Music is always the language in which one can converse with the beyond.' For Beethoven, 'only art and science can raise men to the level of gods'; while for Schoenberg, 'Music conveys a prophetic message revealing a higher form of life towards which mankind evolves.' For Fauré, the emotion produced by sound, rather than a set of philosophical beliefs, is the starting point, but for him too, music's ability to take the listener beyond everyday life is fundamental. His musings are prompted by the memory of the distant tolling of evening bells:

An incident such as this does in fact frequently promote a torpid state of mind, and a very agreeable one, in which thoughts merge imperceptibly into each other. Are we at this moment reaching out to that other world? This is in fact where music begins.[26]

Each of these composers, in a slightly different way, expresses the idea that music can *communicate with* whatever is beyond everyday life: the gods, the other world, the higher life. Others have gone still further, and suggested that music can *convey an image* of that 'beyond', that paradise. Liszt, in typically extravagant terms, wrote that:

> On the wings of the infinite art [music] draws us with it to regions into which it alone can penetrate, where, in the ringing ether, the heart expands and, in anticipation, shares in an immaterial, incorporeal, spiritual life . . . that takes hold of us and sweeps us into the turbulent maelstrom of the passions which carries us out of the world into the harbour of a more beautiful life.[27]

For him, music does not simply tantalize the listener with glimpses of the beyond: it has the power to take him there. Hindemith, too, suggests that music, at its best, can transform the world, and its human inhabitants with it:

> Harmonic . . . melodic and rhythmic laws, as worked out in a beautiful and most exalted composition, would transform the world's woes and falsehood into the ideal habitat for human beings, who by the same process of musical ennoblement would have grown into creatures worthy of such a paradise.[28]

Busoni shares Hindemith's view that music's ultimate goal is to convey an idea of paradise, even if that goal is almost never realized: 'Mankind will never know the essence of music in its reality and entirety.' However, the ideal comes closest to achievement – for Busoni, as for most musicians – in the music of Mozart:

From the depths of our hearts, therefore, let us be thankful to the select few who are privileged, at least on a small scale, through taste and form, inspiration and mastery, to set up a miniature model of that sphere from which all beauty and power flow to them.[29]

Busoni, Hindemith and Liszt share a belief that music, in its most ideal form, can convey an idea of 'paradise': an idea that has clear associations with Christianity. The language used by all three, however, is spiritual rather than religious. Specific Christian beliefs are not necessary in order to understand the idea of 'paradise' that they invoke: it may equally be interpreted as a generalized human aspiration. Some composers present their ideals in religious terms, others in secular, 'earthly' terms; perhaps the more important point is the common ground all these composers share. 'Paradise in music' is an inclusive ideal: it has appealed to composers without clear religious convictions, as well as to those for whom religious faith is the central fact in their life.

For those composers in the latter group, however, the divine is not merely the ultimate aspiration of the process of composition: it is also frequently an active component of it. Many composers – very diverse in other ways – have expressed the belief that they are directly assisted in their work by God. Haydn wrote that 'If my composing is not proceeding so well, I walk up and down the room with my rosary in my hand, say several Aves, and then ideas come to me again.' He was humble in his belief that God, rather than he himself, deserved the gratitude of the listeners. When receiving public acclaim during a performance of *The Creation*, he gestured heavenwards and declared that 'It comes from there.' He often inscribed his scores with the words *Soli Dei Gloria* – to God alone be the glory. Many other composers have marked their scores similarly: Mozart, Weber, Bruckner, Dvořák, Elgar, Liszt, Messiaen, Stravinsky and Stockhausen, for example. Numerous composers have believed that their musical achievements were essentially a divine gift: 'a good theme is a gift from God' (Brahms), 'the gift was from above' (Weber), 'it is the greatest gift of the divinity and cannot be compared with anything else' (Richard Strauss). Others have understood themselves as working in collaboration with the divine. Beethoven wrote that 'I must leave behind me what the Eternal Spirit has infused into my soul and bids me complete', while Schoenberg wrote:

> Has the Lord granted to a [musical] thinker a brain of unusual power? Or did the Lord silently assist him now and then with a bit of his own thinking? From my own experience I know that [thematic unity] can be a subconsciously received gift from the Supreme Commander.[30]

For such composers, the communication of a vision of paradise is the ultimate goal of music. The composer is the prophet, responsible for guiding mankind on the long and sometimes treacherous road to religious revelation. The composer himself may not know exactly the route that he is taking, but he is guided by his faith in the rightness of his ultimate destination. Mahler – who declared that 'all my works are an anticipation of the life to come' – described this process:

> Like a somnambulist he [the composer] wanders towards them [goals] – he doesn't know which road he is following (it may skirt dizzy abysses) but he walks toward the distant light, whether this be the eternally shining stars or an enticing will-o'-the-wisp.[31]

Schubert, too, described the ultimate goal of his work as a distant light. Great works of art, he wrote, 'show us in the darkness of this life a bright, clear, lovely distance, for which we may hope with confidence . . . Blissful moments brighten this dark life; up there these blissful moments become continual joy, and happier ones still will turn into visions of yet happier worlds.' For Schoenberg, the responsibility of conveying such visions was profound and never ending – it was passed on from generation to generation of composers:

There is only one content, which all great men wish to express: the longing of mankind for its future form, for an immortal soul, for dissolution into the universe – the longing of this soul for its God. This alone, though reached by many different roads and detours, and expressed by many different means, is the content of the works of the great; and with all their strength, with all their will they yearn for it so long and desire it so intensely until it is accomplished. And this longing is transmitted with its full intensity from the predecessor to the successor, and the successor continues not only the content but also the intensity, adding proportionately to his heritage.[32]

Schoenberg's prophecy has proved correct: composers right up to the present day have continued the attempt to communicate a vision of paradise in their music. It is somewhat invidious here to single out examples, but one piece from recent years in particular may be mentioned, since it seems to epitomize its composer's entire career. Messiaen strove throughout his life to convey his religious faith in his music: he wrote that 'to raise upon the mountain the doors of our prison of flesh, to give our century the spring water for which it thirsts, there shall have to be a great artist who will be both a great artisan and a great Christian'. His *Eclairs sur l'au-delà* (*Glimpses of the Beyond*) was first performed in New York in 1992, six months after his death. It presents a series of eleven visions of the Beyond, each accompanied by a biblical epigraph, mostly from the Book of Revelation. As such it seems to sum up Messiaen's religious faith: it takes up the theme of paradise explored in works such as *L'Ascension, Couleurs de la cité céleste* and *Des canyons aux étoiles*, and makes it the entire focus of the eighty-minute work. Musically, too, it draws on techniques from Messiaen's entire career: the use of birdsong, the non-directional structures, the seemingly endless melodies, the exotic orchestration and huge percussion section are all familiar from earlier works, but are combined in this final piece in an entirely fresh way. It is a magnificent fulfilment of what George Benjamin described as his teacher's 'purpose in life': 'to communicate the revelation of eternal beauty to a modern world in a modern way'.

Messiaen's paradise is a specifically Christian – indeed, Catholic – vision, but belief in the possibility of 'paradise in music' is by no means confined to composers with religious convictions. Many have asserted music's capacity to reveal spiritual truth from outside the boundaries of orthodox belief. This view was propounded more vigorously by Wagner than by any other composer. Towards the end of his life, he controversially developed the idea of 'art-religion', claiming that music drama could produce a spiritual response in its audience. He increasingly came to disdain the organized Christian church, believing that 'Religion . . . lives, but only at its primal source and sole true dwelling-place, within the deepest, holiest inner chamber of the Individual.' It was in this innermost recess of the individual that music too could take effect. Using the metaphor of a 'sea of harmony', he claimed that only the human heart could perceive its true depths:

> The eye knows but the surface of this sea; its depth the depth of heart alone can fathom . . . Man dives into this sea, only to give himself once more, refreshed and radiant, to the light of day. His heart feels widened wondrously, when he peers down into this depth, pregnant with unimaginable possibilities whose bottom his eye shall never plumb, whose seeming bottomlessness thus fills him with sense of marvel and the presage of Infinity. It is the depth and infinity of Nature herself, who veils from the prying eye of Man the unfathomable womb of her eternal Seed-time, her Begetting, and her Yearning . . . This Nature is, however, none other than the nature of the human heart itself, which holds within its shrine the feelings of desire and love in their most infinite capacity.[33]

For Wagner, the infinite and the ideal were held within the human being, even if they were seldom identified: the musical paradise he proclaimed was thus attainable, if only theoretically, within the earthly life, rather than being the life-after-death proposed by Christianity. This vision of an earthly paradise, attainable through music, has been shared by many composers. Liszt, for example, quoted E. T. A. Hoffmann's words with approval:

> To Hoffmann, music revealed 'that faraway country which surrounds us often with the strangest presentiments and from which wondrous voices call down to us, waking all the echoes that sleep in our restricted breasts, which echoes, awakened now, shoot joyfully and gladly up, as though in fiery rays, making us sharers in the bliss of that paradise'.[34]

For Debussy, too, music was the means of revealing a magical realm, belonging to the real world but seldom perceived by it:

> It is music alone that has the power to evoke imaginary scenes at will, to conjure up the intangible world of fantasies secretly shrouded within the mysterious poetry of the night, the thousand indistinguishable noises made by moonbeams caressing the leaves.[35]

Schubert had a vision of a music that could convey an earthly paradise, as he described in his account of a dream of a mysterious funeral ritual:

> Before I was aware of it, I found myself in the circle, which uttered a wondrously lovely sound, and I felt as though eternal bliss were gathered together into a single moment.[36]

And Berlioz, too, dreamt of music's capacity to create an earthly bliss beyond all others, as he wrote to Ferrand in 1858: 'Last night I dreamt of music, this morning I recalled it all and fell into one of those supernal ecstasies.'

The belief in a paradise attainable on earth through music has never been expressed more strongly than in the Romantic tradition, and it may be argued that no work within that tradition proclaims a love for an idealized earth more strongly than Mahler's *Das Lied von der Erde*. For Mahler in this work, Eden is not a far-off land: on the contrary it exists on earth – it is the earth transfigured. At the end of the final movement, 'Das Abschied', Mahler expresses his love of this idealized earth by adding these words to the text he sets:

> Everywhere the lovely earth blossoms forth in spring
> And grows green anew.

Everywhere, for ever, horizons are blue and bright,
For ever . . . ever . . .

All notes gradually disappear during these words except the
pentatonic scale on which the work is based; and this (itself
tonally ambiguous, lacking fourth and seventh) fades gradually into utter stillness. The agonized, pessimistic emotions
expressed throughout the work are 'redeemed' by the final
surrender of the self to the healing power of the natural
world. Music's capacity to represent the ideal – the possibility
of paradise – is asserted at the same time as the individual life
expires. Music's ability to transform the everyday world, by
revealing the paradise that exists both beyond and within it,
is triumphantly proclaimed.

Postscript

As we have seen, there are striking parallels between the ideas of composers from different ages. There is also, however, an intriguing sense that, where inspiration is concerned, each composer is feeling anew 'the air of another planet'. Many of the opinions with which we are now comfortable would have seemed radical and contentious in their own day. Views that now seem orthodox were often constructed in opposition to the too complacent routines of less perceptive colleagues.

The need for a challenge to accepted views is no less vital in our own day. The conditions under which artists work have changed rapidly. The old patriarchal authorities of religion and state, which were formerly passively accepted as a sort of collective super-ego, are now dying. Moreover, the way in which we understand ourselves is changing. Until recently, mechanistic assumptions prevailed: that we were in complete control of our own minds, that we were separate from matter, which was mechanically obedient to its own laws. Both these assumptions now seem too rigid, too simple.

Our age, too, must generate the new from within itself. Increasingly, there is an understanding that we are inseparably connected, as humans, to the rest of nature: it is the duty of artists to provide a response to this. We must find our new morals and mores within, but this means that the darkness, violence, animality and fear that are also within must be fully faced. These tendencies can no longer be labelled as 'evil', and simply set aside without further inspection. If we are to understand with full subtlety what it is to be, then we must open ourselves to uncertainty, to empathy with people and the natural world around us, as they appear to us inwardly and intuitively.

Too often, our age has artificially suppressed pain, suffering, and evil: it has justly been called the Aspirin Age. This age must die: the dark side must be acknowledged. Artists usually understand such things deeply. That is why much contemporary art seems to be concerned with suffering, even violence and destruction, to an extent that is otherwise unaccountable. People ask why: why more suffering? They believe that the depiction of evil itself causes suffering, and object to this. But the answer is that precisely the opposite is true: suffering encountered in art or ritual is *healing*. If we give ourselves to the experience of the art, fully and fearlessly, we are journeying inward to our truth, from where we will find our new world. The famous gap between modernist composer and audience is founded on nothing more than this misunderstanding.

At the climax of my opera *Inquest of Love* (1992), which is really an inquest into the suffering caused by illusory love, I wrote the affirmative words 'O Love-filled Light! O healing Love!', words sung over and over again, to a blaze of sound. The music then gradually subsides, away from that 'sacred marriage' scene: we return to the old Abbot, alone and back in his monastery. He sings the words 'I saw – O Grace-given ecstasy – Your boundless love . . . that You will bring, in time, all to eternal bliss. Grant, O Light, that the last dividing veil of illusion soon be torn away.' The Abbot is in meditation, just as he was at the beginning of the opera. In one sense the whole opera in between may be understood as his work of art, divinely delivered to him by means of a state of inner concentration. The suffering – depicted by some of the darkest music I have written – has given a glimpse of a redeemed world. But it is only a glimpse – the resolution is only partial. The Abbot too realizes that there are veils of illusion still to be torn away, but he now sees them in a clearer light.

I see, looking back, that this theme – suffering and healing – has been my own most common source of musical inspiration. Looking within, often with the use of external triggers, I seek this *vision of healing,* which is embodied in the forms of light's energy and love's connectedness. But looking within also forces one to encounter all the terrors of darkness. It is as if, instead of dealing with a patriarchal God of controlling authority, one now meets a Goddess in all her unpredictability: fluid, instinctual, affirming what is. She magnificently dares one to become aware of one's depth, and of life as an undivided whole.

This 'Goddess' has seemed to appear in many guises in my work. She might appear as the Virgin Mary of *Madonna of Winter and Spring* (1986), a lengthy orchestral work where the electronics enhance the numinosity of the textures of dark winter and radiant spring. Or she might be Jesus in *Passion and Resurrection* (1981), a church opera: Jesus' music heals, bringing together the hard and dark music of the crucifixion, dominated by priest and soldier, with the anguished and lyrical love of the three Marys. She is present in *Soleil noir/Chitra* for ensemble (1995), which presents Gérard de Nerval's depression and insanity (as interpreted in Julia Kristeva's study of melancholia, *Soleil noir*) alongside its polar opposite: Rabindranath Tagore's representation of the Princess Chitra from the *Mahabharata*, an innocently pre-Freudian, but equally profound, representation. The two 'selves', equally valid in our time, find a synthesis – though the gap between them is initially immense. There is a 'maternal' presence, too, in *Hidden Voice (1)* for ensemble (1996). This piece tries to represent the secret 'mother's voice' for which we long through all time, eternally seeking, of which Baudelaire spoke in 'L'Invitation au voyage':

> Tout y parlerait
> À l'âme en secret
> Sa douce langue natale.

Sweet voiced, the violin, viola and cello are all muted, half hidden amidst the ensemble.

In *Scena* for violin and chamber ensemble (1992), the protagonist–violin goes through a series of transformations, the biggest of which occurs after the dark opening 'Lament' when, in the next section, 'Mystical Event', two woodwind enter for the first time with flying figures suggesting mythological birds. The violin then puts on his mute and plays extremely high music, softly and slowly for a long time, in stark contrast to the energetic dissonances of the previous music. The work has been aptly likened to a *Bildungsroman*, a type of nineteenth-century novel where the hero or heroine is psychologically metamorphosed.

The darkness is still blacker in a work for soprano, piano and tape, *Nachtlied*, which I wrote after teaching a course on music and the Holocaust. I heard that Goethe's 'Wanderers Nachtlied' ('Über allen Gipfeln ist Ruh') was written in a little hunting lodge on the site of what was to become the infamous Buchenwald. The Nazis respectfully preserved the lodge, piling irony on tragedy. I visited the site and noticed the eerie stillness that Goethe felt: 'No birds were singing.' I took that poem and confronted it with two meditations by

Rudolf Steiner, on light and darkness, day and night, 'normal' and spiritual worlds. I always felt, even many years before this experience, that Goethe (and Schubert in his setting) was writing about death.

Intimations of death are among those darknesses encountered on the journey within, of course. But death in this journey – as in my music – has usually appeared as a transformation, not as an ending, though it remains terrifying none the less. A work such as *Death of Light/Light of Death*, the quintet on Grünewald's *Crucifixion*, to which I have already referred, tries to enter deeply into the frightening desolation of the racked body on the cross, and the utter débâcle that this sight represents to those around. But the second part of the title, *Light of Death*, refers to the famed healing qualities of the picture. Death can offer an illuminating guide to our understanding of our wholeness, force us to accept (as sometimes happens on the death of a close friend or relative) that there is, at the very least, a deep mystery within. More powerfully still, it can be a pointer to the undivided light. John the Baptist on the right of the picture clearly understands this.

Many religions encourage meditations on death. One of my favourite Buddhist meditations involves imagining one's death as a process of dissolving the outer world in light, then incorporating that light (just one's body alone in empty space), melting the body to the size of a small Sanskrit letter in the heart region, and dissolving that letter in seven stages, while visualizing different textures and colours said to occur during the dying process, until all has gone. There is no Jonathan Harvey left. Only consciousness, empty of attributes. The clear light that may arise at this point is the place of healing, where all clinging and self-grasping have ceased. If such a state is maintained, one has attained liberation, that of which the 'douce langue natale' has always been singing.

This liberation from the fear of death is, more importantly, a platform from which we can act to heal others. It is also an emptiness which connects us without barriers to others, experiencing their suffering, joining them across their separateness. In the same way, a piece of music can unify contrasting light and darkness, consonance and dissonance, high and low in one greater harmony – while using 'just notes', empty of inherent existence: intensely vivid, yet paradoxically having only the existence we impose on them with our minds.

This state of liberation, of emptiness, of healing, is a new world for me, and it represents a profound source of inspiration. I gain further understanding of this new world, and further inspiration, from books, art, meditation, dreams, reflections of the inner self in landscape and nature, and many other sources. Each of my pieces is a somewhat faltering attempt to draw out a certain aspect of this new world, to share with an audience what I hope will give them happiness, however much that may mean encountering pain in the process.

In previous periods, the sensations I am experiencing would probably have been described as the inspiration of God, or of a mysterious unconscious. It is possible that, in the future, they will be understood along the lines I have described – or along some other lines, appropriate for our culture and our age. Inspiration cannot remain constant: each composer must discover it anew.

Notes

ONE The Composer and the Unconscious

Epigraph. Karlheinz Stockhausen, *Stockhausen on Music*, ed. Robin Maconie, London, Marion Boyars, 1989, p. 36.

1 Tchaikovsky, letter to Mme von Meck, 24 June 1878. (A convenient source for this fascinating series of letters is David Brown, *Tchaikovsky: A Biographical and Critical Study*, vol. II: *The Crisis Years (1874–78)*, London, Gollancz, 1982, chapter 6.)

2 Mahler, letter to Anna Bahr-Mildenburg, 18 July 1896.

3 Quoted in Etienne Gilson, *Choir of Muses*, trans. M. Ward, London, Sheed and Ward, 1953, p. 180.

4 Quoted in Josiah Fisk (ed.), *Composers on Music: Eight Centuries of Writing*, Boston, North Eastern University Press, 1997, p. 235.

5 Quoted in Elliott Schwartz and Barney Childs (eds.), *Contemporary Composers on Contemporary Music*, New York, Holt, Rinehart and Winston, 1967, p. 192.

6 Quoted in Meirion and Susie Harries, *A Pilgrim Soul: The Life and Work of Elisabeth Lutyens*, London, Michael Joseph, 1989, p. 110.

7 Arnold Schoenberg, *Style and Idea*, New York, trans. D. Newlin, London, Williams and Norgate, 1951, p. 166.

8 Emily Anderson (ed.), *Letters of Mozart and his Family*, London, Macmillan, 1938, no. 586.

9 Mahler, letter to his wife, 8 June 1910, translated in Alma Mahler, *Gustav Mahler: Memories and Letters,* ed. Donald Mitchell and

Knud Martner, 4th edn, London, Cardinal, 1990, p. 328.

10 Max Maria von Weber, *Carl Maria von Weber*, London, 1865, p. 368.

11 Quoted in Evelyn Underhill, *Mysticism*, London, Methuen, 1911, p. 395.

12 Quoted in Sam Morgenstern (ed.), *Composers on Music*, London, Faber and Faber, 1958, p. 295.

13 Arthur Honegger, *Je suis compositeur*, Paris, 1951, introduction.

14 Tchaikovsky, letter to Mme von Meck, 24 June 1878.

15 Richard Wagner, *Richard Wagner's Prose Works*, trans. William Ashton Ellis, London, Kegan Paul, Trench, Trübner and Co., 1892–9, vol. II, p. 13.

16 *Revue SIM*, Paris, 15 March 1912.

17 Quoted in Fisk (ed.), *Composers on Music*, p. 215.

18 Honegger, *Je suis compositeur*, chapter VIII.

19 Debussy, letter to Raoul Bardac, 31 August 1901, translated in Edward Lockspeiser (ed.), *The Literary Clef*, London, John Calder, 1958, p. 110.

20 Quoted in Morgenstern, *Composers on Music*, p. 312.

21 Quoted in R. J. Buckley, *Sir Edward Elgar*, London, John Lane, 1905, p. 75.

22 Max Maria von Weber, *Carl Maria von Weber*.

23 André-Ernest-Modeste Grétry, *Mémoires*, Paris, 1789.

24 *Richard Wagner's Prose Works*, vol. vi, p. 170.

25 Leoš Janáček, *Letters and Reminiscences*, ed. Bohumir Štědroň, trans. G. Thomsen, Prague, Artia, 1955, p. 188.

26 Hans Werner Henze, *Bohemian Fifths: An Autobiography*, London, Faber and Faber, 1998, p. 482.

27 Debussy, letter to André Messager, 12 September 1903.

28 Gabriel Fauré, letter to his wife, 21 September 1904, translated in Lockspeiser (ed.), *The Literary Clef*, pp. 145–6.

29 Quoted in J. A. Fuller-Maitland, *Brahms*, London, Methuen, 1911, pp. 69–70.

30 Richard Strauss, *Recollections and Reflections*, ed. W. Schuh, trans. L. J. Lawrence, London, Boosey and Hawkes, 1953, p. 114.

31 Conversation with Natalie Bauer-Lechner, 1896, quoted in Dika Newlin, *Bruckner, Mahler, Schoenberg*, New York, King's Crown Press, 1947, p. 165.

32 Mahler, letter to Anton Seidl, 17 February 1897.

33 Pyotr Ilyich Tchaikovsky, *The Diaries of Tchaikovsky*, trans. Wladimir Lakond, Westport, Conn., Greenwood Press, 1973.

34 Anton von Webern, *The Path to the New Music*, ed. W. Reich, trans. L. Black, London, Universal Edition, 1975, p. 37.

35 Bálint András Varga, *Conversations with Iannis Xenakis*, London, Faber and Faber, 1996, p. 61.

36 Paul Griffiths, *New Sounds, New Personalities: British Composers of the 1980s in Conversation with Paul Griffiths*, London, Faber and Faber, 1985, p. 31.

37 Vernon Gotwals (ed.), *Joseph Haydn: Eighteenth Century Gentleman and Genius* (a translation of contemporary memoirs of Haydn by Griesinger and Dies), Madison, University of Wisconsin Press, 1963, p. 61.

38 Robert Schumann, *On Music and Musicians*, ed. Konrad Wolff, trans. P. Rosenfeld, London, Dennis Dobson, 1947, p. 36.

39 Igor Stravinsky, *Poetics of Music*, trans. A. Knodel and I. Dahl, Cambridge, Mass., Harvard University Press, 1947, p. 55.

40 György Ligeti, *György Ligeti in Conversation*, London, Eulenberg, 1983, p. 124.

41 Griffiths, *New Sounds, New Personalities*, p. 56.

42 Quoted in Fisk (ed.), *Composers on Music*, p. 56.

43 Igor Stravinsky, *An Autobiography*, New York, Norton, 1962, p. 31.

44 Brian Ferneyhough, *Collected Writings,* ed. James Boros and Richard Toop, Amsterdam, Harwood Academic Publishers, 1995, p. 260.

45 Tchaikovsky, letter to Mme von Meck, 24 June 1878.

46 Leoš Janáček, *Janáček's Uncollected Essays on Music*, ed. Mirka Zemanova, London, Marion Boyars, 1989, p. 72.

47 Carlos Chávez, *Musical Thought*, Cambridge, Mass., Harvard University Press, 1961, p. 30.

48 Gotwals (ed.), *Joseph Haydn*, p. 141.

49 Debussy, letter to Pierre Louÿs, 22 January 1895.

50 Nicolai Rimsky-Korsakov, *My Musical Life*, ed. C. Van Vechten, trans. J. A. Joffe, London, Martin Secker, 1924, p. 193.

51 Roger Sessions, 'The Composer and his Message', in A. Centano (ed.), *The Intent of the Artist*, Princeton, 1941, p. 101.

52 Honegger, *Je suis compositeur*, chapter VIII.

53 Arnold Schoenberg, *Style and Idea*, pp. 18, 102.

two The Composer and Experience

Epigraph. György Ligeti, *György Ligeti in Conversation*, London, Eulenberg, 1983, p. 20.

1 Charles Ives, 'Essays Before a Sonata', in *Three Classics in the Aesthetic of Music*, New York, Dover, 1962, p. 156.

2 Robert Schumann, *On Music and Musicians*, ed. Konrad Wolff, trans. P. Rosenfeld, London, Dennis Dobson, 1947, p. 181.

3 Quoted in Sam Morgenstern, *Composers on Music*, London, Faber and Faber, 1958, p. 74.

4 Emily Anderson (ed.), *The Letters of Beethoven*, London, Macmillan, 1961, p. 258.

5 Schumann, *On Music and Musicians*, p. 258.

6 Claude Debussy, *Debussy on Music*, ed. and trans. Richard Langham Smith, New York, Knopf, 1977, p. 118.

7 Busoni, interview with reporter, 1911.

8 Quoted in Marghanita Laski, *Ecstasy*, London, The Cresset Press, 1961, p. 106.

9 Quoted in Donald Mitchell, *Gustav Mahler, The Wunderhorn Years*, London, Faber and Faber, 1975, p. 342.

10 Leoš Janáček, *Letters and Reminiscences*, ed. Bohumir Štědroň, trans. G. Thomsen, Prague, Artia, 1955, p. 90.

11 Richard Wagner, *Richard Wagner's Prose Works*, trans. William Ashton Ellis, London, Kegan Paul, Trench, Trübner and Co., 1892–9, vol. II, p. 307.

12 Thea Musgrave, 'The Decision', *Musical Times*, CVIII, 1967, pp. 988–91.

13 Schumann, *On Music and Musicians*, p. 260.

14 Schoenberg, letter to Helen Heffernan, 19 September 1942.

15 Michael Tippett, 'The Birth of an Opera', in *Moving Into Aquarius*, revised edn, London, Paladin, 1974, p. 55.

16 Hector Berlioz, *Selected Letters*, ed. Hugh Macdonald, London, Faber and Faber, 1995, p. 169.

17 Gluck, dedicatory letter to Grand Duke Leopold of Toscana, December 1767.

18 Roland-Manuel (ed.), 'Une esquisse autobiographique de Maurice Ravel', *Revue Musicale*, 1938, no. 187, p. 17.

19 Quoted in Nicholas John (ed.), *Opera Guide: Debussy, Pelléas et Mélisande*, London, John Calder, 1982, p. 13.

20 Richard Strauss, *Recollections and Reflections*, ed. W. Schuh, trans. L. J. Lawrence, London, Boosey and Hawkes, 1953, p. 154.

21 Mendelssohn, conversation with Lobe, quoted in Percy A. Scholes (ed.), *Oxford Companion to Music*, 8th edn, London, Oxford University Press, 1953, p. 199.

22 Franz Liszt, 'Berlioz and his *Harold* Symphony', translated in Oliver Strunk (ed.), *Source Readings in Music History*, London, Faber and Faber, 1952, pp. 863, 866.

23 Hector Berlioz, *Memoirs*, trans. David Cairns, London, Granada, 1970, pp. 109–10.

24 Schoenberg, programme note to *Das Buch der hängenden Gärten*, trans. Hans Keller.

25 Schoenberg, letter to Richard Dehmel, 13 December 1912.

26 Igor Stravinsky, *Chronicle of My Life*, London, Victor Gollancz, 1936, p. 137.

27 Ibid., p. 171.

28 Pierre Boulez, sleeve note to his own CBS recording of *Pli selon pli*, trans. Felix Aprahamian.

29 Mendelssohn, letter dated 16 October 1830.

30 Quoted in Carol Neuls-Bates (ed.), *Women in Music*, New York, Harper and Row, 1982, p. 157.

31 Bartók, autobiographical article of 1921, reprinted in *Tempo*, no. 13, 1939.

32 Ibid.

33 Debussy, letter to Ernest Chausson, 2 October 1893, in Claude Debussy, *Letters*, ed. François Lesure, trans. Roger Nichols, London, Faber and Faber, 1987, p. 54.

34 Igor Stravinsky, *Memories and Commentaries*, London, Faber and Faber, 1960, p. 110.

35 Ligeti, *György Ligeti in Conversation*, pp. 22–3.

36 Stravinsky, *Chronicle of My Life*.

37 Mendelssohn, letter dated August 1831.

38 Emily Anderson (ed.), *Letters of Mozart and his Family*, London, Macmillan, 1938, no. 219.

39 Bedřich Smetana, *Letters and Reminiscences*, ed. F. Bartoš, trans. D. Rusbridge, Prague, Artia, 1955, p. 190.

40 Leoš Janáček, *Intimate Letters*, trans. and ed. John Tyrrell, London, Faber and Faber, 1994, p. 196.

41 Ibid., p. 230.

42 Wagner, *Richard Wagner's Prose Works*, vol. I, p. 322.

43 Carlos Chávez, *Musical Thought*, Cambridge, Mass., Harvard University Press, 1961, p. 5.

44 Max Maria von Weber, *Carl Maria von Weber*, London, 1865, preface.

45 Mahler, quoted in the *Manchester Guardian*, 2 February 1957.

46 Wagner, *Richard Wagner's Prose Works*, vol. I, p. 73.

47 Wilhelm Furtwängler, *Notebooks 1924–54*, trans. Shaun Whiteside, rev. edn, London, Quartet, 1995, p. 147.

48 Paul Hindemith, *A Composer's World*, Cambridge, Mass., Harvard University Press, 1952, p. 62.

49 Arnold Schoenberg, *Style and Idea*, trans. D. Newlin, London, Williams and Norgate, 1951, p. 108.

50 Ibid., p. 156.

51 Ravel, 'On Inspiration', letter to *The Chesterian*, IX, January 1928.

52 Schumann, *On Music and Musicians*, p. 78.

53 Tchaikovsky, letter to Mme von Meck, 24 June 1878.

54 Berlioz, letter to Princess Carolyne Sayne-Wittgenstein, 12 August 1856.

55 Richard Strauss, quoted in *Oxford Companion to Music*, 8th edn, p. 202.

56 Quoted in Josiah Fisk (ed.), *Composers on Music: Eight Centuries of Writing*, Boston, North Eastern University Press, 1997, pp. 410–11.

57 Igor Stravinsky, *Poetics of Music*, trans. A. Knodel and I. Dahl, Cambridge, Mass., Harvard University Press, 1947, p. 50.

THREE The Composer and the Audience

Epigraph. Benjamin Britten, 'On Receiving the First Aspen Award'. Text quoted in full in Elliott Schwartz and Barney Childs (eds.), *Contemporary Composers on Contemporary Music*, New York, Holt, Rinehart and Winston, 1967, pp. 116–23.

1 Ralph Vaughan Williams, *National Music and Other Essays*, 2nd edn, Oxford, Oxford University Press, 1987, p. 3.

2 Igor Stravinsky, *Poetics of Music*, trans. A. Knodel and I. Dahl, Cambridge, Mass., Harvard University Press, 1947, p. 141.

3 Aaron Copland, *Music and Imagination*, Cambridge, Mass., Harvard University Press, 1952, p. 47.

4 Emily Anderson (ed.), *Letters of Mozart and his Family*, London, Macmillan, 1938, no. 411.

5 Vernon Gotwals (ed.), *Joseph Haydn: Eighteenth Century Gentleman and Genius*, Madison, University of Wisconsin Press, 1963, p. 33.

6 Richard Wagner, *Richard Wagner's Prose Works*, trans. William Ashton Ellis, London, Kegan Paul, Trench, Trübner and Co., 1892–9, vol. I, p. 301.

7 Richard Strauss, letter to Hofmannsthal, 22 October 1907.

8 Arthur Honegger, *Je suis compositeur*, Paris, 1951, chapter VIII.

9 Charles E. Ives, *Memos*, ed. John Kirkpatrick, London, Calder and Boyars, 1973, p. 131.

10 Quoted in Josiah Fisk (ed.), *Composers on Music: Eight Centuries of Writing*, Boston, North Eastern University Press, 1997, p. 39.

11 Gluck, dedicatory preface to *Alceste*.

12 H. C. Robbins Landon, *The Collected Correspondence and London Notebooks of Joseph Haydn,* London, Barrie and Rockliff, 1959, p. 209.

13 Emily Anderson (ed.), *The Letters of Beethoven*, London, Macmillan, 1961, p. 334.

14 Aaron Copland, 'Autobiographical Sketch', from *Our New Music*, New York, Whittlesey House, 1941.

15 Robert Schumann, *On Music and Musicians*, ed. Konrad Wolff, trans. P. Rosenfeld, London, Dennis Dobson, 1947, p. 247.

16 Michael Tippett, *Tippett on Music*, ed. Meirion Bowen, Oxford, Clarendon, 1995, p. 280.

17 Arnold Schoenberg, *Letters*, ed. Erwin Stein, trans. E. Wilkins and E. Kaiser, London, Faber and Faber, 1964, p. 54.

18 Ibid., p. 243.

19 Ibid., p. 290.

20 Arnold Schoenberg, *Style and Idea*, trans. D. Newlin, London, Williams and Norgate, 1951, p. 55.

21 Quoted in Schwartz and Childs (eds.), *Contemporary Composers on Contemporary Music*, p. 244.

22 Brian Ferneyhough, *Collected Writings,* ed. James Boros and Richard Toop, Amsterdam, Harwood Academic Publishers, 1995, p. 243.

23 Pierre Boulez, *Orientations*, trans. Martin Cooper, London, Faber and Faber, 1986, p. 481.

24 Mya Tannenbaum, *Conversations with Stockhausen*, trans. David Butchart, Oxford, Clarendon, 1987, pp. 37–8.

25 Bálint András Varga, *Conversations with Iannis Xenakis*, London, Faber and Faber, 1996, pp. 97–8.

26 Ibid.

27 Allen Edwards, *Flawed Words and Stubborn Sounds: A Conversation with Elliott Carter*, New York, Norton, 1971, p. 89.

28 Wagner, *Richard Wagner's Prose Works*, vol I, p. 327.

29 Quoted in David Brown, *Tchaikovsky: A Biographical and Critical Study*, vol. IV, *The Final Years (1885–93)*, London, Gollancz, 1991, pp. 287–8.

30 Wagner, *Richard Wagner's Prose Works*, vol IV: 'To the Kingly Friend', pp. 1–2.

31 Tippett, *Tippett on Music*, p. 281.

32 Wagner, letter to Franz Liszt, October 1849.

33 Leoš Janáček, *Intimate Letters*, trans. and ed. John Tyrrell, London, Faber and Faber, 1994, p. 185.

34 Wagner, letter to Mathilde Wesendonck, dated St Sylvester's Day, 1857.

35 Mahler, letter to his wife, 4 September 1910, translated in Alma Mahler, *Gustav Mahler: Memories and Letters*, ed. Donald Mitchell and Knud Martner, 4th edn, London, Cardinal, 1990, p. 335.

36 Hector Berlioz, *Memoirs*, trans. David Cairns, London, Granada, 1970, p. 42.

37 Ibid., p. 622.

38 Ibid., pp. 633–4.

39 Wagner, *Richard Wagner's Prose Works*, vol. I, p. 357.

40 Quoted in Brown, *Tchaikovsky*, London, Gollancz, 1982, vol. II, pp. 233–4.

41 Nicolai Rimsky-Korsakov, *My Musical Life*, ed. C. Van Vechten, trans. J. A. Joffe, London, Martin Secker, 1924, pp. 201, 193.

42 Vaughan Williams, *National Music and Other Essays*, p. 9.

43 Quoted in Schwartz and Childs (eds.), *Contemporary Composers on Contemporary Music*, pp. 116–23.

44 Wagner, *Richard Wagner's Prose Works*, vol. I, p. 73.

45 Copland, *Music and Imagination*, p. 111.

46 Paul Hindemith, *A Composer's World*, Cambridge, Mass., Harvard University Press, 1952, p. 5.

47 Pierre Boulez, 'Sonate que me veux-tu?', *Perspectives on New Music*, spring 1963.

48 Luciano Berio, 'Poesia e musica – un "esperienza"', in *Incantri Musicali*, no. 3, August 1959.

49 Wagner, *Richard Wagner's Prose Works*, vol. III, p. 278.

50 Olivier Messiaen, in Claude Samuel, *Conversations with Olivier Messiaen*, trans. F. Aprahamian, London, Stainer and Bell, 1976, p. 11.

51 Quoted in Sam Morgenstern, *Composers on Music*, London, Faber and Faber, 1958, p. 205.

52 Friedrich Nietzsche, *The Birth of Tragedy*, ed. O. Levy, trans. W. A. Haussmann, Edinburgh, Foulis, 1909, pp. 128–9.

53 Martin Cooper, 'Scriabin's Mystical Beliefs', *Music and Letters*, XVI, 1935, p. 110.

54 Wagner, *Richard Wagner's Prose Works*, vol. 1, p. 357.

55 Anderson (ed.), *The Letters of Beethoven*, p. 1405.

FOUR The Composer and the Ideal

Epigraph. Michael Tippett, *Tippett on Music*, ed. Meirion Bowen, Oxford, Clarendon, 1995, p. 6.

1 Ibid., p. 13.

2 Igor Stravinsky, *An Autobiography*, New York, Norton, 1962, pp. 113, 14.

3 Igor Stravinsky, *Poetics of Music*, trans. A. Knodel and I. Dahl, Cambridge, Mass., Harvard University Press, 1947, p. 51.

4 Igor Stravinsky, *Memories and Commentaries*, London, Faber and Faber, 1960, p. 106.

5 *George Benjamin*, London, Faber and Faber, 1997, pp. 23–4.

6 Richard Strauss, *Recollections and Reflections,* ed. W. Schuh, trans. L. J. Lawrence, London, Boosey and Hawkes, 1953, p. 76.

7 Stravinsky, *An Autobiography*, p. 54.

8 Ferruccio Busoni, 'Sketch of a New Aesthetic of Music', in *Three Classics in the Aesthetic of Music*, New York, Dover, 1962, p. 81.

9 Aaron Copland, 'Music as an Aspect of the Human Spirit', in *Copland on Music*, New York, André Deutsch, 1960.

10 Arnold Schoenberg, 'Composition with Twelve Tones', in *Style and Idea*, trans. D. Newlin, London, Williams and Norgate, 1951, p. 113.

11 Franz Liszt, 'Berlioz and his *Harold* Symphony', translated in Oliver Strunk (ed.), *Source Readings in Music History*, London, Faber and Faber, 1952, p. 854.

12 Stravinsky, *Poetics of Music*, pp. 141–2.

13 Ralph Vaughan Williams, *National Music and Other Essays*, 2nd edn, Oxford, Oxford University Press, 1987.

14 Paul Hindemith, *A Composer's World*, Cambridge, Mass., Harvard University Press, 1952, closing words.

15 Verdi, letter to V. Torrelli, 23 December 1867.

16 Mahler, letter to Steiner, 17 June 1879.

17 Emily Anderson (ed.), *The Letters of Beethoven*, London, Macmillan, 1961, p. 633.

18 O. E. Deutsch (ed.), *Schubert: A Documentary Biography*, trans. E. Blom, London, Dent, 1946, section on 1824, 'lost notebook'.

19 Anderson (ed.), *The Letters of Beethoven*, pp. 804, 254.

20 Deutsch (ed.), *Schubert: A Documentary Biography*, section on 1823, 'My Prayer'.

21 Tippett, *Tippett on Music*, p. 293.

22 Mahler, letter to his wife, 11 September 1908, translated in Alma Mahler, *Gustav Mahler: Memories and Letters,* ed. Donald Mitchell and Knud Martner, 4th edn, London, Cardinal, 1990, p. 305.

23 Berlioz, quoted in Pierre Boulez, *Orientations*, trans. Martin Cooper, London, Faber and Faber, 1986, p. 217.

24 Claude Debussy, *Debussy on Music*, ed. and trans. Richard Langham Smith, New York, Knopf, 1977, p. 93.

25 Mya Tannenbaum, *Conversations with Stockhausen*, trans. David Butchart, Oxford, Clarendon, 1987, p. 29.

26 Gabriel Fauré, letter to his wife, 11 September 1906, translated in Edward Lockspeiser (ed.), *The Literary Clef*, London, John Calder, 1958, p. 149.

27 Liszt, 'Berlioz and his *Harold* Symphony', translated in Strunk, *Source Readings in Music History*, p. 850.

28 Hindemith, *A Composer's World*, p. 102.

29 Ferruccio Busoni, *The Essence of Music*, trans. R. Ley, London, Rockliff, 1957, p. 200.

30 Schoenberg, *Style and Idea*, pp. 71, 109.

31 Mahler, letter to Anton Seidl, 17 February 1897.

32 Schoenberg, *Style and Idea*, p. 26.

33 Richard Wagner, *Richard Wagner's Prose Works*, trans. William Ashton Ellis, London, Kegan Paul, Trench, Trübner and Co., 1892–9, vol. I, p. 112.

34 Liszt, 'Berlioz and his *Harold* Symphony', translated in Strunk, *Source Readings in Music History*, p. 851.

35 Debussy, *Debussy on Music*, ed. and trans. Richard Langham Smith, p. 101.

36 Deutsch (ed.), *Schubert: A Documentary Biography*, section on 1822.

Select Bibliography

Anderson, Emily (ed.), *Letters of Mozart and his Family*, London, Macmillan, 1938
- (ed.), *The Letters of Beethoven*, London, Macmillan, 1961
Berlioz, Hector, *Memoirs*, trans. David Cairns, London, Granada, 1970
- *Selected Letters*, ed. Hugh Macdonald, London, Faber and Faber, 1995
Boulez, Pierre, *Orientations*, trans. Martin Cooper, London, Faber and Faber, 1986
Bowra, C. M., *Inspiration and Poetry*, London, Macmillan, 1955
Busoni, Ferruccio, *The Essence of Music*, trans. R. Ley, London, Rockliff, 1957
- 'Sketch of a New Aesthetic of Music', in *Three Classics in the Aesthetic of Music*, New York, Dover, 1962
Chávez, Carlos, *Musical Thought*, Cambridge, Mass., Harvard University Press, 1961
Copland, Aaron, *Music and Imagination*, Cambridge, Mass., Harvard University Press, 1952
Debussy, Claude, *Debussy on Music*, ed. and trans. Richard Langham Smith, New York, Knopf, 1977
- *Letters*, ed. François Lesure, trans. Roger Nichols, London, Faber and Faber, 1987
Deutsch, O. E. (ed.), *Schubert: A Documentary Biography*, trans. E. Blom, London, Dent, 1946

Duchesneau, Louise, *The Voice of the Muse: A Study of the Role of Inspiration in Musical Composition*, Frankfurt-am-Main, Peter Lang, 1986

Ferneyhough, Brian, *Collected Writings,* ed. James Boros and Richard Toop, Amsterdam, Harwood Academic Publishers, 1995

Fisk, Josiah (ed.), *Composers on Music: Eight Centuries of Writing*, Boston, North Eastern University Press, 1997

Griffiths, Paul, *New Sounds, New Personalities: British Composers of the 1980s in Conversation with Paul Griffiths*, London, Faber and Faber, 1985

Harding, Rosamond E. M., *An Anatomy of Inspiration*, Cambridge, Heffer, 1940

Henze, Hans Werner, *Bohemian Fifths: An Autobiography*, London, Faber and Faber, 1998

Hindemith, Paul, *A Composer's World*, Cambridge, Mass., Harvard University Press, 1952

Honegger, Arthur, *Je suis compositeur*, Paris, 1951

Ives, Charles, 'Essays Before a Sonata', in *Three Classics in the Aesthetic of Music*, New York, Dover, 1962

Janáček, Leoš, *Intimate Letters*, trans. and ed. John Tyrrell, London, Faber and Faber, 1994

Koestler, Arthur, *The Act of Creation*, London, Hutchinson, 1964

Landon, H. C. Robbins, *The Collected Correspondence and London Notebooks of Joseph Haydn*, London, Barrie and Rockliff, 1959

Laski, Marghanita, *Ecstasy*, London, The Cresset Press, 1961

Ligeti, György, *György Ligeti in Conversation*, London, Eulenberg, 1983

Lockspeiser, Edward (ed.), *The Literary Clef*, London, John Calder, 1958

Mahler, Alma, *Gustav Mahler: Memories and Letters*, ed. Donald Mitchell and Knud Martner, 4th edn, London, Cardinal, 1990

Morgenstern, Sam (ed.), *Composers on Music*, London, Faber and Faber, 1958

Neuls-Bates, Carol (ed.), *Women in Music*, New York, Harper and Row, 1982

Rimsky-Korsakov, Nicolai, *My Musical Life*, ed. C. Van Vechten, trans. J. A. Joffe, London, Martin Secker, 1924

Schoenberg, Arnold, *Style and Idea*, trans. D. Newlin, London, Williams and Norgate, 1951

Schumann, Robert, *On Music and Musicians*, ed. Konrad Wolff, trans. P. Rosenfeld, London, Dennis Dobson, 1947

Schwartz, Elliott and Barney Childs (eds.), *Contemporary Composers on Contemporary Music*, New York, Holt, Rinehart and Winston, 1967

Stockhausen, Karlheinz, *Stockhausen on Music*, ed. Robin Maconie, London, Marion Boyars, 1989

Storr, Anthony, *The Dynamics of Creation*, Harmondsworth, Penguin, 1976

Strauss, Richard, *Recollections and Reflections*, ed. W. Schuh, trans. L. J. Lawrence, London, Boosey and Hawkes, 1953

Stravinsky, Igor, *Poetics of Music*, trans. A. Knodel and I. Dahl, Cambridge, Mass., Harvard University Press, 1947

– *An Autobiography*, New York, Norton, 1962

Strunk, Oliver, (ed.), *Source Readings in Music History*, London, Faber and Faber, 1952

Tannenbaum, Mya, *Conversations with Stockhausen*, trans. David Butchart, Oxford, Clarendon, 1987

Tippett, Michael, *Tippett on Music*, ed. Meirion Bowen, Oxford, Clarendon, 1995

Underhill, Evelyn, *Mysticism*, London, Methuen, 1911

Varga, Bálint András, *Conversations with Iannis Xenakis*, London, Faber and Faber, 1996

Vaughan Williams, Ralph, *National Music and Other Essays*, 2nd edn, Oxford, Oxford University Press, 1987

Wagner, Richard, *Richard Wagner's Prose Works*, trans. William Ashton Ellis, 8 vols., London, Kegan Paul, Trench, Trübner and Co., 1892–9

Weber, Max Maria von, *Carl Maria von Weber*, London, 1865

Webern, Anton von, *The Path to the New Music*, ed. W. Reich, trans. L. Black, London, Universal Edition, 1975

Index